Enduring Hope

The Impact of the
Ramallah Friends Schools

By Patricia Edwards-Konic

Max Carter, Contributing Editor

Friends United Press
Richmond, Indiana • www.fum.org/shop

Enduring Hope: The Impact of the Ramallah Friends Schools

Copyright © 2008 by Friends United Press

Friends United Press
101 Quaker Hill Drive
Richmond IN 47374
friendspress@fum.org
www.fum.org/shop

Cover photo courtesy of Joyce Ajlouny
Back cover photo courtesy of Patricia Edwards-Konic

Library of Congress Cataloging-in-Publication Data

Edwards-Konic, Patricia, 1948-
  Enduring hope : the impact of the Ramallah Friends Schools / by Patricia Edwards-Konic ; Max Carter, contributing editor.
      p. cm.
  ISBN 978-0-944350-71-3 (pbk. : alk. paper)
  1. Madaris al-Frindz (Ram Allah) 2. Society of Friends--Education--West Bank--Ramallah. 3. Ramallah--Social conditions. I. Carter, Max. II. Title.
  LC571.E39 2008
  370.95695--dc22
                            2008027499

Dedication

To all the former and current students, teachers, and staff
of the Ramallah Friends Schools,
for their dedication, their courage, and their commitment

Table of Contents

Foreword

In the summer of 2007, Violet Zaru, a pillar of the Ramallah Quaker community, passed away in her mid-eighties. Born shortly after World War I and the defeat of the Ottoman Turks who had occupied the region for five hundred years, Violet grew up under the British Mandate in Palestine. As a young educator, she began her career during the Jordanian occupation of the West Bank, following the withdrawal of the British and the 1948 war which led to the establishment of the modern state of Israel. Approaching the culmination of her professional life in 1967, she experienced Israel's occupation of Ramallah, along with the West Bank and Gaza. During her retirement years, she saw the advent of the Palestinian Authority in 1995 and the removal of Israeli troops from the city.

Violet lived in one place through her nine decades on earth but under four different governments and in a culture still influenced deeply by a fifth—the Ottomans. Throughout that time, there was at least one constant in her life and in Ramallah: the Quaker community and the Friends Schools.

This is one of the great contributions of Friends in that part of the Middle East—stability. In a region where the only constant is said to be change, the Ramallah Friends Schools have been another constant, a steady presence since the 1860s. Occupying powers come and go; national alignments wax and wane; Israel and Palestine are in and out of the spotlight. But the Friends

Schools continue, year in and year out, to educate young people and wield a valued influence.

In a much less dramatic way, the Ramallah Friends Schools have wielded their influence on me. As a boy growing up in Indiana during the 1950s and 1960s, Carter family gatherings often featured my grandfather's reading of letters from his sister, Annice Carter, who served for many years as the principal of the Friends Girls School (FGS) in Ramallah. My world of dairy cows and cornfields was expanded through those missives which evoked exotic places and biblical stories.

I came to have my own experience in Ramallah when I declared my status as a conscientious objector to military service and was given permission by my draft board to find my own site for alternate service. Majoring in education studies at university and wanting to apply my training and my commitment to peacemaking in an area challenged by conflict, I chose to teach at the Friends Boys School (FBS) and performed my two-year obligation there from 1970-72.

In spite of Friends United Meeting's best efforts to orient me and other volunteers in their mission programs, I arrived in Ramallah during August of 1970 woefully naïve and uninformed. Only three years removed from the still vivid recollection of Israel's seemingly miraculous victory in the six day war, my only context for understanding the Middle East was Hollywood movies such as *Exodus*, the biblical image of David versus Goliath, and American culture's lack of knowledge about the Arab world. I was in for a rude awakening!

Within weeks of my arrival, the Palestine Liberation Organization (PLO) had hijacked four airliners into the Jordanian and Egyptian desert and was holding the passengers and crew hostage. My students at FBS approached me on the playground and asked, "Mr. Carter, what do you think of the hijacking?" I gave the expected response of pleading Quaker pacifism. I remember being taken aback by their response:

"We don't want to see any violence or harm done to people, either. But the world doesn't recognize the Palestinian people; all they understand is violence; we have to get the world's attention."

Within the next few weeks, "Black September" broke out in Jordan, and my students stayed awake at night listening to radio accounts of what might be happening to their relatives during the fighting between the forces of the PLO and King Hussein. Then Gamal Abdul Nasser, President of Egypt, died unexpectedly and the region was thrown into deep unease while the war of attrition between the Arab nations and Israel continued.

Through it all, members of the Palestinian Quaker community, my fellow teachers, and my students gave me a primer in the history, politics, and culture of the area. Listening to Israeli radio, traveling in Israel, and becoming acquainted with Israeli and Jewish perspectives all added further nuance to my awakening. Everything was revelation, and on one memorable school day. I had another opening, courtesy of my students.

School was about to be dismissed for the Muslim holiday of Eid il-Miraj, and, unfamiliar with Islam, I asked one of my Muslim students to explain. Omar said, "The feast commemorates the Prophet Muhammad's miraculous escape from enemies when his horse flew him to safety in Jerusalem."

"Yeah, sure!" Kameel, a Christian student, blurted out. "A horse sprouted wings and flew off to Jerusalem. You expect us to believe that?"

Without hesitation, Omar responded, "And Jesus walked on water?"

Suddenly, I gained a valuable insight. The miracles in the Bible were true for me; I had not questioned them. Walking on water, turning water into wine, multiplying loaves and fishes, rising from the dead ... all were part of a narrative that informed my own story. But there are other narratives, other stories that are held with equal truth and which form others' self-understanding.

"The central truth of the Israeli/Palestinian conflict," says
Naomi Chazan, former deputy speaker of Israel's Parliament—
the Knesset—"is that there are two narratives that are equally
true for both sides, and they don't meet."

One of the great contributions of the Friends Schools and the
Quaker community in Ramallah is that Friends education takes
seriously the narrative of other communities. Whether articulated as "that light which illumines every human in the world"
(John 1:9), "that of God in every person" (George Fox), or "that
principle which is pure and proceeds from God, confined to no
religion nor excluded from any" (John Woolman), Quakerism is
noted for recognizing, in Robert Barclay's terms, that the human
experience of God's salvation is not limited to one particular set
of terms—but rather in the *experience* of that light and life and
power which those terms signify.

My experience in Ramallah changed me and formed me in
very important ways, not the least of which was in the recognition of the importance of "the others'" narrative of their experience. I cherish that knowledge.

As witnessed in the lives of graduates of the Ramallah Friends
Schools—and in the influence of the Schools on Palestinian society—the Quaker presence in Palestine since the mid-nineteenth
century is a treasure to be cherished and celebrated. Generations
of alumni, informed by the Quaker ethos of the Schools, have
gone on to lead meaningful lives, contributing in important ways
to the religious, social, economic, and political life of the region
and beyond.

This brief book, offering but a small glimpse into the sig-
nificance of that presence and contribution, performs a valuable
function even beyond that of informing readers about the thrill-
ing story of Friends in Palestine. It offers an enduring hope in a
very dark time: the hope of endurance, of lives deeply formed by
the Christian witness to peace, justice, and reconciliation which
Friends embrace, of principles that can be embodied in institu-

tions. The author demonstrates through the words of those who have come under the influence of the Ramallah Friends Schools that the Quaker ethos there is a "treasure in earthen vessels" that should be celebrated.

Only two years before her death, I heard Violet Zaru comment, "When I get to heaven, I have only one thing I want to say to God: next time you create a world, don't put your two favorite children on the same piece of ground!"

Violet's whole life was spent seeking a way to reconcile people who were in conflict—in the classroom, in the religious community, and at the Friends Play Center in the Amari refugee camp. Her beloved Ramallah Friends Schools embody the same desire. Now Violet is in the presence of God, and I trust that she's got the ear of the Divine and is sharing her concern.

The Friends Schools, meanwhile, have the ear of 1,100 students and a significant portion of Palestinian society, continuing to offer a Quaker education in the midst of that conflict. With this book, I hope that the ears—and eyes, minds, and hearts—of many more are reached by the important narrative of the Schools as one vital story among so many others.

Max L. Carter
April, 2008

Introduction

Sybil and Eli Jones left New England in 1867 to travel to the Holy Land, resulting in the opening of Ramallah Friends Schools. Sybil was fifty-nine, the same age I was 140 years later when I undertook my journey to be Friend in Residence at the Friends Schools.

When I first visited Ramallah Friends Schools (RFS) in December 2005, I was impressed. I could feel the impact of the Schools as I visited with alumni and others who were influenced by the school. After returning to the United States, I mentioned often that someone needed to write a book about the impact of the Friends Schools. And here I was, in spring of 2007, to do just that!

I found Ramallah to be an amazing place, but also a difficult place. Amazing as I was embraced by so many people on the streets, in cafes, and on the school grounds, with, "Welcome! Welcome!" Difficult when I heard gunfire at night, or watched how hard it was for families to live, what we would call, a "normal" life.

The Friends Schools are placed on either side of bustling, downtown Ramallah. Catching a taxi was easy, and the drivers all knew where the Friends Schools were. No extra directions were needed, just the words, "Friends Schools." Residents were glad to see an American who was unafraid to walk their streets and be a part of their daily lives, who was willing to assist in their school.

When I would strike up a conversation with someone on the street, one of their first questions would be to ask why I was in Ramallah. When I told them I was Friend in Residence at RFS, they would break out in smiles and say, "Welcome! Welcome!"

Abe in the vegetable market was always on the lookout for me. He wanted to be a translator for me, and certainly helped in the marketplace. This Muslim man knew he could trust me because I was a Quaker and because I was connected with the Ramallah Friends Schools. Over and over I found the same thing. As a Christian woman walking and shopping alone, I was safe and welcomed! And introductory conversations often led to faith conversations.

One of my most memorable days in Ramallah came early in my stay. I received a phone call around eleven in the morning from Joyce Ajlouny, director of the Ramallah Friends Schools. "I have your first interview for the book. Do you remember 'Peter, Paul and Mary,'" she asked.

"Of course," I replied. They were one of my all-time favorite groups. "Why?"

"Peter Yarrow will be here at two today to meet with a small group. Would you like to join us?"

Along with Paul McCartney, he was top on my list of people I would like to meet, so it was a no-brainer to say, "Yes!"

Peter entered with a huge smile and his guitar, which he immediately pulled out and began singing, "Don't Laugh at Me." I was the only one singing along (under my breath) until he asked us all to join in. It was the theme song of his organization, "Operation Respect."

We sang "Puff, The Magic Dragon," "Blowing in the Wind," and several other songs as he explained "Operation Respect." Over the past nine years, he has worked as an organizer, as well as a performer, to bring respect into the classrooms of America.

Working closely with "Educators for Social Responsibility," their goal has been to train teachers and administrators to resolve conflict creatively. They are teaching educators to create a safe environment of mutual dialogue and making choices based on nonviolent conflict resolution. Music and the arts are key elements of the program. Over forty thousand people have been trained in the program to date.

As we sang with Peter and learned some new songs, it was illustrated how music speaks louder than words and can create a climate of understanding and respect. As a Jew, he is working for peace by translating this program into Arabic for schools in Palestine; he asked if he could bring trainers back to the Ramallah Friends Schools when it was completed. The director and board members immediately accepted his generous offer.

Peter Yarrow was just one in a long line of famous people who came to assist Ramallah Friends Schools in some way. The values he brought with him: respect, nonviolent conflict resolution, music, the arts, and all things creative, mesh perfectly with the ideals of RFS, as I hope you will get a sense of from this book.

Later in my stay in Ramallah I attended English Day and Music Day performances at RFS. English Day is an opportunity for students to show off their English. As I sat listening to each class, enjoying their dances, their songs, and what they had learned, I realized I understood every word! Their fluency in English left me awestruck as I realized it was their second language! How different the Music Day performances were—they were mostly in Arabic—but music transcended the language barrier and I enjoyed every minute of it!

The three months I spent at the Ramallah Friends Schools were some of the best times of my life. I learned so much. I was cared for and supported. I met so many amazing new people. I learned to live in an occupied land. I walked in the paths of our biblical ancestors. My heart is full of joy. What an awesome God we serve!

I would like to thank everyone who participated in this project. The staff of Ramallah Friends Schools assisted me in so many special ways, including housing and assistance for the research component of the project. The responders to the questionnaires and those I interviewed provided valuable insights. The Friends United Meeting staff in Richmond, Indiana, provided support with my regular work assignments. The readers who took time from their schedules to read the draft and supply comments— Joyce Ajlouny, Max Carter, Retha McCutchen, and Colin South—this project is better because of your collaboration. And finally, my two Ramallah families, the Izmeknehs, who adopted me and provided me with love and many new experiences, and Joyce Ajlouny and Ziad Khalaf and their sons, who encouraged me to "pass by" often. Plus many thanks and love to my husband, Dan, who supported and encouraged me to do this project, and my sons, Mike and Rick, who said, "Go for it, Mom!" Without your help this project would not have been possible.

Chapter 1
Foundation of Hope

A question frequently asked of those in the middle of the Israeli-Palestinian conflict is "Do you see any hope?" Response to that query takes many forms. For those involved with the long history of the Ramallah Friends Schools, hope also takes many forms, not the least of which is the impact which Friends education has already had in preparing the ground for a better future. It is noteworthy, then, that the story of the Quaker schools in Palestine begins with the Hope School.

Hope School opened its doors in Ramallah in 1869. Its goal was to educate girls, who up to that date had no hope for an education. This is the story of enduring hope in Ramallah through the Friends Schools and the impact they have made.

Ramallah, a small village established in the early 1500s by Christian Arabs, was visited in 1869 by Eli and Sybil Jones of New England Yearly Meeting. This was their second trip to the Middle East and their first to Ramallah. Amazingly, when they arrived, they met Jacob Hishmeh who spoke English. As they held their meetings for worship and shared the love and hope of Christ, Jacob translated.

Following a preaching meeting for women that Sybil led, fifteen-year-old Miriam Karam met Eli on the streets. Miriam asked if a school for girls could be opened and she volunteered to be the first teacher. As the Jones' left the area to go north to Lebanon, they left money with Jacob Hishmeh to open the girls school with Miriam as teacher. Hope School opened in August 1869 with twenty girls.

Friends Schools became pioneers in women's education as they opened four additional day schools in other villages for a total of fifty girls attending. Jacob Hishmeh fought for the opportunity for girls to go to school and visited homes to convince parents their daughters needed education. Jacob's niece, Sabha Hishmeh was one of the first students, and later became a teacher. He supervised these growing schools for seventeen years before moving to Jerusalem.

From Day School to Boarding School

As the evangelical movement took hold among Gurneyite Friends, yearly meetings began to explore mission opportunities around the world. At the Richmond (Indiana) Conference of 1887, mission work was an important topic of discussion.

For twenty years, Friends in New England and Britain had financially supported the schools in Ramallah and the Brummana School in Lebanon. In 1889 British Friends proposed that New England Yearly Meeting assume full responsibility for the schools in Ramallah, and Britain would assume responsibility for Brummana. The proposal was approved and the transfer of property was undertaken.

The transfer marked the beginning date of the Friends Girls School (FGS) as a boarding school, which brought girls from all over Palestine, with some of the teachers coming from Lebanon. The idea was to find girls from different villages who could attend FGS and later return to their home villages as teachers. To find families progressive enough to allow their daughters to attend the school, representatives of FGS had to travel far and wide through what was then known as Greater Syria. This was a pioneering idea to spread education for girls throughout the region.

FGS opened with fifteen girls plus staff. The furnishing for the traditional stone house, which was expanded into the school building, came by boat to Jaffa and then to Ramallah by camels. Katie Gabriel came from Lebanon to be the first headmistress and stayed for the next forty years, retiring in 1929.

Ramallah in 1889 had a resident population of 3,000 people, mainly Christians. It was the center of a sixty-six village district; only six of which were Christian. All were small, tribal, and supported by sustainable agrarian practices which had changed little since the time of Jesus. An unforeseen development occurred as girls from around the region came to go to school in Ramallah.

Christina Jones writes in *Friends in Palestine*:

> At that time, villages in Palestine had little social interchange with one another and townspeople knew little of the life of the villagers. By introducing families from a number of towns and villages from other parts of the country into the relative privacy of the girls boarding school, Palestine learned of the beauty and healthful air of the hill country town, 2,850 feet above sea level. ... As a result, Ramallah was to grow into a summer resort, attracting people from all walks of life. Their coming opened up a new world to the inhabitants, especially after the first World War, which was to bring tremendous changes in the life of the people and to mark great developments in the service Friends would render in the Holy Land in the coming years. (8)

Friends Boys School Opens

In 1892 a report was sent to New England Yearly Meeting asking for a school for boys, "Now that the people of Ramallah have seen the good affect Christianity and education is having upon their daughters, they are asking the same blessing for their sons."

Enough money was collected by the Christian Endeavor Union of New England Yearly Meeting by the spring of 1901 to send Elihu and Almy Chase Grant to open a school for boys. By October 1, 1901, fifteen boys began their education at the Friends Boys School (FBS), located in former homes near the Friends Girls School. The students were all from Ramallah, except one, and ranged in age from seven to fifteen. In 1906, the first students graduated.

Timothy Hussey, a Friend from New England, negotiated with numerous landowners for a fourteen acre tract of land in Ramallah's neighboring village of El-Bireh for the expansion of the boys school. The land was purchased in 1905, and permission to build was finally received in 1913. A year later the substantial two-and-a-half story stone building was ready for students.

First World War and British Mandate

The new school had barely been readied for use when World War I erupted. Both schools were closed during the war. The first occupants of the new building were forces of the Ottoman Turkish military, the new kitchen and dining hall serving as a stable for horses. In January 1915 the Americans at the school returned to the United States. Three American Friends returned to Ramallah through the Red Cross in June 1918.

The girls school had a small number of soldiers billeted there but no horses, so the damage was less. The Friends meetinghouse had been used as a canteen by the occupying British forces after the defeat of the Turks. Local legend tells of a thousand liquor bottles being cleaned out of the 1910 meetinghouse at war's end! Friends continued to meet for worship in the home of Elias and Emily Audi throughout these difficult years. It would not be the last time that war would interrupt the work of Friends to educate the youth of the area.

The schools reopened in October 1919. FGS was fortunate to have the steady hands of Principal Alice Jones, Katie Gabriel and her two nieces, and other former teachers return. Thirty boarding students and ten day students enrolled.

FBS was not as fortunate; there were no returning staff. Edward and Miriam Kelsey from New England set about getting the school ready. Farid Tabri was hired to teach Arabic, and other new teachers were added. There were thirty-seven boarding students and thirty-three day students.

Christina Jones writes, "The first ten years after the war were ones of hope and promise in Palestine. ... this optimism was reflected in the school in Ramallah as well as the country as a whole" (69).

But changes were coming in the region which would impact not only the schools and local residents, but the whole world. In response to the tenuous situation which Jews often experienced in the Diaspora, a movement known as Zionism emerged in late nineteenth century Europe. The goal of Zionism was the creation of a Jewish homeland. Soon the focus of this effort centered on Palestine and efforts were made to begin nation-building through purchase of land, emigration, and establishment of collective farms.

Pronouncements were made by the British during WWI to win Jewish and Arab support—each group promised homelands to be liberated from Ottoman rule. Meanwhile, the British and French secretly divided the Middle East into mandates for themselves, with the British occupying Palestine after the war. Jewish nation-building continued, and Arab nationalism grew. Tensions between the two erupted in 1929 with much violence and hundreds killed. The late 1930s saw a protracted Arab revolt as Jewish emigration increased, and then WWII broke out.

The Friends Schools remained open, even amid the tensions. The first Palestinian principal of the Friends Boys School was Khalil Totah, who served until 1944 when he moved with his family to the United States.

When Willard and Christina Jones arrived to assume leadership, they were welcomed by friends in the community. She wrote, "In speeches of welcome the villagers paid a beautiful tribute to the Friends Mission for all it had brought to Palestine, [and] to Ramallah in particular ... they spoke of how the coming of these Friends opened up the village to the rest of the country. Contrasting it with another village not too far away, they remarked that Ramallah might have remained like it if the schools had not been built" (91-92).

The Partition of Palestine

With the end of the war, Jewish and Arab national aspirations resumed, leading to continued violence. The British, faced with mounting attacks on soldiers and civilians, announced their intention to vacate their mandate in 1948, asking the United Nations to plan for what might come afterwards. A partition plan was devised which would give a Jewish state fifty-six percent of Palestine, with an Arab state to be created out of the remaining forty-four percent. Israel declared its independence in May 1948, and war immediately erupted again.

The year 1948 was a difficult one. Hundreds of thousands of Palestinian Arabs fled the new state of Israel and the additional twenty-two percent of Palestine that was conquered by Israel in the fighting. Some left voluntarily; others were forced out by the fighting. Thousands flooded into Ramallah, and the schools and meetinghouse opened their doors to help. The meetinghouse became home to several families, with curtains subdividing the worship room. Many boarding students were withdrawn from the school as parents were concerned for their safety. "Ramallah was fast becoming a 'City of Refuge,'" (105) wrote Christina Jones. Commencement was held early because the stability of the area was undermined by the massacre in the Arab village of Deir Yasin (ten miles away, near Jerusalem) and as thousands of refugees continued to flee from the area partitioned as Israel.

"The role of Quakers in Palestine is important. In 1948 they were the only ones with an infrastructure in place that could help during the refugee crisis. Instead of leaving, they stayed, helped and kept the Friends Schools open," stated Dr. Adel Yahya, director of PACE (Palestinian Association for Cultural Exchange) and the parent of a seventh grade girl at FBS. "The impact of Friends is felt by almost everyone. Out of all the other denominations, Quakers have contributed the most, especially in Ramallah."

1967 War and Israeli Occupation

With the armistice of 1949, Ramallah was left significantly changed. The original families were outnumbered by displaced Palestinians; refugee camps were established in and around the town; Jordan occupied the West Bank and educational authority was transferred to Amman. A war of attrition continued between Israel and the surrounding Arab nations. The Suez crisis of 1956, refusal of the Arab nations to recognize Israel, Israel's refusal to recognize Palestinian Arabs, and the growing hostility on both sides all contributed to the six day war of 1967. Through this period, the Friends Schools grew, however. Students came from throughout the region and all over the West Bank for the excellent education offered. Quaker leadership was strong, with Mildred White, Anna Langston, Annice Carter, and Kenneth Shirk serving as principals at the girls school; Willard Jones, Robert Bassett, Delbert Reynolds, George Sherer, Harold Smuck, and Lloyd Brightman headed the boys school.

In June of 1967, Ramallah and the Friends Schools were irreversibly altered by the war. Israel launched a pre-emptive strike on Egypt and Syria, and Jordan entered the war. While King Hussein of Jordan encouraged Palestinian residents of the West Bank to "fight with your teeth and fingernails," he removed troops to Jordan, leaving only a token force. Israel swiftly occupied the entire West Bank, including Ramallah, and set up a military government.

At the boys school, Palestinian Quaker and pharmacist Fuad Zaru was named principal during this difficult time. At the girls school, a new principal, Peggy Paull, had been named. Under the new circumstances, Friends United Meeting (FUM) called Annice Carter out of retirement to aid in the transition. Early in her new residency at the school, Annice was preparing for bed when she heard gunfire. Going to the balcony outside her apartment, she saw a jeep full of Israeli soldiers, firing their weapons into the tree tops.

"What are you doing down there," Annice yelled down. "We're firing our guns into the trees!" was one soldiers' response. "I can see that," Annice replied. "Now stop it! You're scaring my girls," she went on. "Turn your jeep around; drive through the front gate; and close the gate behind you!" And they did.

"Before the 1967 war," recalled Ziad Khalaf, a 1974 graduate living in Ramallah, "there was pride in the school and classes were full. The thirty-three students in my class came from Amman, the Gulf, the widespread Palestinian community, and the American community in Jerusalem. When we returned to school after the war, there were now nine students in my class."

The boarding students from throughout the Middle East did not return, and there was consideration of closing the schools. The decision was made to reopen them as day schools for students in the area. Jean Zaru, wife of the new FBS principal, stated that she and her husband were instrumental in keeping the school going after the 1967 war. "I taught for fourteen years," she said, "and developed an ethics curriculum that was considered by the State Department of Education. Fuad taught and was FBS principal for the next eighteen years." As wife of the school principal, Jean also sometimes had to host the Israeli military governor of the West Bank and other officials of the occupying power in the principal's home. In a message once shared in meeting for worship, Jean spoke of what a challenge it was to offer her best chocolate cake to these men—but that it was her Christian obligation to "love the enemy," as Jesus had commanded.

Most classes were not co-educational until after the 1967 war. Mazen Karam, a 1971 graduate, stated, "We were the guinea pigs. They tried co-ed classes in my eighth grade; it didn't work. In eleventh grade, boys took Arabic at FGS and girls came to FBS for sixth to eighth periods. When I graduated it was fully co-educational, but it took four years to work it out." A system was finally devised through which the girls school became the "arts school," and the boys school became the "science and math" campus. Boys wishing a less challenging academic load would go to the girls school in eleventh and twelfth grades to take that curriculum. Similarly, girls wanting a greater challenge would go to the boys school for their junior and senior year. Max Carter, a teacher at the boys school from 1970-72, tells of the year when six girls arrived in his junior math class. After the first week, they came to him and pleaded to be sent back to the girls school; they couldn't handle the work, they said. "Give it until the first test," Carter asked of them. When the results of that first test came back, the girls occupied five of the top six positions in the class. They stayed.

After singing the school song, Mazen said, "The sign over the FBS administration building door states it all for me. 'Education is a cutting sword to ignorance; Education is a bright light that stamps out darkness.'" These are words from the school song written by Farid Tabri which they often sang in chapel.

"RFS was a beautiful part of my life," reminisced Issa Cook, a 1954 graduate now living in Houston, Texas. Because of its elevation and cool summer breezes, wonderful restaurants, greenery, and renowned beauty, Ramallah before the 1967 war was a vacation spot for many in Arab lands throughout the Middle East. "I really miss those days. Until the occupation in 1967, Ramallah was called 'The Bride of Palestine.' I was the deputy mayor at that time. It was a happy city until the occupation came.

"I will never abandon nor forget the school. I will always be there for it, both me and my children. We (Palestine) have a choice—either death or education. I want to work more on scholarships to help educate those in Ramallah. Through education, we can get justice for Palestine."

Intifadas

Growing frustration among Palestinians reached a boiling point by 1987, with the failure of the international community to address the ongoing Occupation and development by Israel of a matrix of control over the West Bank and Gaza. The first years of the Occupation in Ramallah had been relatively quiet; residents were in a state of shock and denial and responded by adopting an attitude of mourning: no celebrations, no expressions of their culture of dance and the arts, and no violent response to the Occupation. It had been assumed that matters would be redressed by the United Nations, by the PLO (Palestine Liberation Organization), by somebody. That somebody turned out to be the Palestinian citizenry themselves.

The first Intifada (1987-93)—an Arabic word meaning "uprising" or "shaking off"—was a spontaneous explosion of popular resistance to the Israeli Occupation, and ended when the Oslo Accord was signed in September 1993.

"I attended RFS during some of the most difficult times," wrote Majeed G. Makhlouf, a 1994 graduate living in Cleveland,

Ohio, where he works as an attorney. "I was in my early teens when the first Intifada began, and Ramallah Friends Schools (RFS) were closed down. I was there during the Gulf War. Despite all these difficulties, RFS made sure that we succeeded and did everything possible to help us through some very difficult periods."

During this time, few visitors stopped by Ramallah Friends Schools, but one such visitor was Fr. James A. Rude SJ, who was teaching high school in Sacramento, California. He wrote, "I did visit it [RFS] once way back in 1992 and I was tremendously impressed with the principal, Khalil Mahshi, and the work they were trying to do despite the actions of the Knesset at that time." He forwarded his observations written in the school newspaper, *The Plank*, about his 1992 visit:

> It had been snowing the day we were there and things looked white and beautiful, if a bit slushy, and everything had stopped—but not because of the snow. Outside the city we too were stopped at a military checkpoint, and it took all our doing as Americans to get through. We finally got in and went to the high school where we met Khalil Mahshi, the principal. The school is over a hundred years old, founded by the Quakers. Khalil told us how the Israelis had for months closed all the Palestinian schools as one way to control the people and dishearten them. In the words of an American psychiatrist who has worked in Gaza, a part of the Occupied Territories, "The strength of the Palestinian people is in their education, and the Israeli government understands this."
>
> As principal, Khalil organized his teachers to meet with groups of students in their homes, since the

Israelis would not let them come to school. But then
the Israelis forbade the home meetings, so Khalil
got his teachers to prepare lesson plans to distribute
to the students' homes. Then the government found
a way to forbid that, too. They obviously want to
destroy the Palestinian culture and their incredible
sense of themselves as a people.

Often the Israelis will arrest students during final
exam prep time or during the exams themselves,
which are the only way for Palestinians to gain ad-
mission to the universities. "If they can't take the
exam," he concluded, "they have to wait a whole
year to try again."

Another visitor during this time was Max Carter, a former
teacher, who returned for three weeks in the summer of 1988 and
noted the eruption of Palestinian pride, the reclaiming of their
cultural celebrations, the "Intifada gardens" that had been planted to provide independence from Israel's agricultural markets,
the cooperative economic and political ventures that had been
started, and the development of a new attitude towards recognizing Israel and promoting a two-state solution to the conflict.
Palestinians were taking control of their own destiny, and social
relationships, attitudes about authority, and many traditional values were being challenged.

During these times when the schools were closed, Quaker
values encouraged the administration to care for the teachers and
staff. Friends Schools teachers were paid, even when the schools
were closed; they were the only school to pay teachers during
this time. These policies and procedures offered hope to the staff
during very difficult days.

The school lost one third of its days and, since it was illegal
for Palestinians to go to school, the educational network went

underground to teach and keep students at grade level. The first year the school was open again all school year was 1995, under the leadership of Retha McCutchen. Her impression was of RFS as "an oasis in the middle of the storm." She served as RFS director from 1995-97, as FUM World Ministries director from 1997-2004 and FUM General Secretary from 1997-2006. She also noted that the schools offered "hope by paying into teachers pensions long before it was the accepted norm in the Palestinian teaching community. RFS [also] set standards for excellence in teaching that later were adopted by government and other private schools."

Following the Oslo Accord and the development of the Palestinian Authority (PA), Israel withdrew troops from selected areas of Palestine, and the Occupied Territories were divided into Zones A, B, and C, with Israel retaining full control of Zone C, joint control with the PA of Zone B, and recognizing full PA autonomy in Zone A. Israel left Ramallah and El-Bireh in 1995, and an economic and social boom erupted for a number of years. Land prices soared astronomically; high rise office buildings rose along Ramallah's main street; optimism was in the air. Ramallah was becoming the de facto capitol of Palestine. But in reality, Israel's matrix of control was tightening. Israeli settlements in the West Bank and Gaza were expanding, and they were being connected by bypass roads that further subdivided the territories. Travel and building permits from Israel were difficult, if not impossible, to come by. The Oslo Accord made a Swiss cheese out of the West Bank, isolating the Palestinian population centers. Optimism began to wane as progress towards an independent Palestinian state was not realized.

As a direct result of the decades of military occupation and increasingly difficult way of life, Palestinian Christians with ties to the West began emigrating in large numbers. From 1967 until today, the percentage of Christians in Palestine declined from seventeen percent to one and a half percent. This affected the

Quaker community, too. Meeting for worship averaged thirty in attendance during the 1970s. By the 1990s, only a handful of Palestinian Quakers remained to conduct the life and worship of the Friends community. Unable to support a pastoral minister, the meeting became unprogrammed; midweek meeting was suspended; the once-flourishing Sunday school was laid down; the meetinghouse itself deteriorated and the tiny congregation moved to a room at the girls school.

A second eruption of Palestinian revolt was inevitable, and the spark that set it off in 2000 was the visit of Israel's controversial figure Ariel Sharon to the Temple Mount/Haram es-Sharif, the third most holy site in Islam. Interpreted widely by Arabs as an attempt to establish Israeli control over the holy site, many Palestinians responded with rock throwing and other acts of violence. The Israeli military responded with force, killing around two dozen Palestinians, and within a few days the first Israeli deaths occurred. The Second Intifada, also known as the al-Aqsa Intifada, had begun. It continued—with far more violence than in the first Intifada—until 2005 and the Sharm el-Sheikh Summit (although those in Hamas and others would say it continues today). The military action continued to affect the lives of the students.

Celine Khoury, a 2005 graduate now studying interior design in Lebanon, wrote:

> I can never forget the day some Israelis were near the school and the school's safety, as well as ours, was threatened. I was in ninth grade and we were in one of our noon classes when we heard the emergency bell ring. Some seniors entered our classroom and asked us to leave the classroom because they were evacuating the whole building. They stood on the bridge between the two buildings where everyone was exposed to the danger area and formed a

cover for the windows, one right next to the other. Students were in lines, and seniors were seen filling the courtyards and forming a path for us to walk through. No one knew what was going on, but everyone felt something was wrong. We reached the science building where we were taken to the lower level.

As soon as I entered there, my heartbeats became so fast, and I sensed some danger. Some students were crying. Others were talking. Some were speechless because of the shock, and some were hugging each other as if they were going apart. Nothing was clear yet, until I heard one girl saying to her best friend, "If anything happens, just know that I love you so much and I don't know what I would have done without you."

I couldn't keep on with their conversation because my own thoughts were emerging now. Hearing students saying that Israelis invaded town and were near the school, I immediately started thinking of my two younger sisters in the FGS. What if Israelis entered there? What will they do? Will one forget the other? How will they manage? How can I contact my parents? All those questions were invading my mind.

I felt scared at that moment, but I was soon surrounded by teachers. Everyone now was inside the hall. The teachers were trying to explain what was happening. A bond between students was immediately felt. Seniors and juniors were sitting with the younger ones. Everyone was together, chattering and trying to make things feel better. Teachers were there for us the whole time. It was scary at the beginning, but it felt extremely safe later on. Parents started coming and picking their children up from the school. Teachers were split; some with the students in the hall and others at the gate of the school checking out the leaving students. Whenever a parent came, they got the student from inside the hall and walked him/her the whole way to the gate, although it isn't much of a distance.

The next thing I remember was a teacher coming to me and taking me to my parents' friend who wanted to drop me at home. Luckily, I reached home safely. I finally saw my sisters whom I was worried about and felt good being home with the whole family. Things got back to normal after some while, and we went back to school. Life continued, but this was one incident that I'm sure many would never forget, including me.

Whenever I remember this story, I remember the students, the teachers, the fear, but most importantly, the care we got from our school and teachers. Since then I truly believed in the saying that "school is our second home." Friends Schools is our second home.

Another alumni in the class of 2005, Ayed O. Ayed, is studying medicine in Amman, Jordan. He remembers the same incident:

"I recall one event that really had an impact on me. It was when the Israeli Army declared an air raid on Ramallah. That day we had school, and everyone was asked to head to the Science Building for safety. Everything seemed chaotic and dreadful. But when all gathered in the building, I felt comforted. I was not alone; students, teachers, and workers were all there. The adults were reassuring us all will be fine as long as we stay together. I realized then the true meaning of 'united we stand.'"

The influence of RFS continued to be important. Colin South, director from 2000-2004, stated, "We were employing over 100 people in the two schools. Throughout the first Intifada salaries were paid to all employees, and even in the worst times of the second Intifada our staff were all paid full salaries with no reductions. ... Every person that you pay has families who depend on what you pay them, so throughout the Intifadas RFS continued to provide a livelihood for its employees."

Following the second Intifada, the schools increasingly drew from the population of the Ramallah/El Bireh area, although they previously had a slightly wider reach into Jerusalem. "The community recognized," continued Colin, "that the school had given status to the town and welcomed that contribution in Ramallah. The history of the school is part of the mythology of the town, so in that respect there was an impact. The school was noticed by the town and was affected by the town."

RFS Impacts the Community

Ramallah Friends Schools "is a tradition," wrote Saleem F. Zaru, a 1977 graduate living in Mt. Airy, Maryland, "a piece of history almost inseparable from the history of Ramallah and Palestine."

The current head of the boys school, Mahmoud Arma, is himself a 1979 FBS graduate. When interviewed, he responded with five ways he sees the Friends Schools impacting the community:

1. Bringing up well-educated children. Over its history we are talking about thousands of graduates who are educated and it is known that most of the students who finish here go on for a college education.

2. Many of the students who go away for college come back and work and serve their country.

3. We believe the school helps the students to become open-minded and they care for their community and for their society. That's why I believe many of our students become leaders of the future.

4. Many students become leaders, either professionally or in other fields such as politics. We have political leaders who have graduated from the school; we have ministers in our government who have graduated from the school; we have people who are leading charity organizations in our society who have also been students at the school.

5. Besides having a good academic program and being willing to explore and experiment with new educational methods, this school is seen as a model school in the field of education. That influence, of course, is throughout the whole educational system. And I know for a fact that in the last ten to fifteen years at least two nongovernmental organizations in the field of education were created as initiatives from the school. The school initiated forming these nongovernmental organizations; hence they are becoming very popular, very active in the field of education.

All of these factors help to keep Palestinians from emigrating and thereby remaining to work and be involved in the country. Joyce Ajlouny, a 1983 graduate and present Friends Schools director, stated:

So many of your Ramallah elite who send their kids here, they have said it time and time again that if it weren't for the Friends Schools they would really be concerned about their children's education and they would probably be leaving. So in a way, Friends Schools is keeping Palestinians put, and by staying here they are helping the economy, the policy making, the decision making, etc. in the country. And it is important that Friends Schools indirectly is taking part in that.

This is a huge impact on the society. I know for sure as a parent if the Friends Schools wasn't here I wouldn't know what to do. Maybe Jerusalem, but who wants to cross checkpoints every day? Because we are American citizens I probably would go back to the States, so the Friends Schools is keeping me here.

And the International Baccalaureate (IB) program has really put this school at a competitive platform with universities around the world. That we are an IB school says a lot. Before, our graduates had a Friends Schools diploma, and for universities abroad, they didn't know what that is. But now when they look at our IB and our scores, they are interested in us.

Hope School of 1869 has grown into a set of schools with international impact. Hope has continued to sprout, spread, and grow in a difficult place, even during hostile events.

Since that time, the Ottomans, the British, the Jordanians, the Israelis, and the Palestinian Authority have held control over Ramallah and El-Bireh. The Friends Schools have been among the few constants—a ray of hope and stability in a dark time.

Chapter 2
Quaker Values

Quaker values are often spoken of as the groundwork of the Ramallah Friends Schools. People in the community recognize that there is something different about RFS and that the difference is rooted in the Schools' Quaker heritage.

Allyn Dhynes taught religion at the girls school from 1997-2000 and is now serving World Vision in Jerusalem. He believes the Quaker witness to its values "is the best way to share Christianity in a non-Christian population. The Light that the Quaker tradition brings to the community comes through time-tested testimonies, love and care extended to them as well, and not through sermons, but by example in an increasingly difficult environment."

Grounded in that, Allyn said, is the "recognition that each child is a child of God—each person has dignity and worth, which is extended to all children." This separates RFS from other schools "because it is rooted in Quaker values ... and all are treated with dignity."

Allyn's wife Holly taught at the boys school during the same time period. She stated, "A small seed or nugget helps them to begin to understand what Quakers understand—every student is valued." Holly used this as the foundation for teaching art in a culture where art is mainly expressed through handicrafts and debka dancing.

This model of a Christian Quaker school grew from its foundations as a Christian school in a Christian village. As the religious culture has changed around it, the majority of the community of Ramallah have at least heard of the school, and even "if they don't know exactly what Quakerism is, they have at least heard the concept and they know about it," states Mahmoud Arma, a 1979 graduate and head of FBS. "When someone asks about this school, they will respond, 'This is a Quaker school.' So this leads many people to ask, 'What is that?' As a result, many people know about Quakerism."

Mahmoud continued, "So we might say this school didn't help in making more people Quakers, in terms of faith, but at least it helped in converting a lot of the beliefs of people in the field of politics, social activity, community, and so on, which I see is very essential and important."

Strategic Planning Articulates Values

For many years, the concern for teaching Quaker values was shared by school directors and staff. But the establishment of such curriculum was always seen as a top-down movement, and ultimately failed. The values were there in the changing culture, but it was hard to teach them.

When Colin South was director from 2000-04, a strategic planning process was implemented. One phase was based on value-driven education. One of the biggest questions was differentiating between Quaker values and those of a western, democratic, liberal education.

Colin stated that there was an "expectation of the parents that there will be discipline, but there will also be freedom of expression, and there will be tolerance. ... I think in the early days of the school it was easier to define the specific Quaker contributions; it is much more difficult to define a specific Quaker contribution in this day and age when there is so much more emphasis on a liberal approach to education, to tolerance, and the value of community."

So a course of action was begun to articulate Quaker values through the strategic planning process. Colin explained it thus:

> We had a Friend who came over from the States whom I had met at Indiana Yearly Meeting, Gary Newton, who was interested in value-driven education. We were interested in trying to identify what were Quaker values and so he came over for a workshop with the staff about faith-driven educational systems. And what came out of that was his request to us to identify what our values were and then critique our whole way of education against those values — to see whether the way in which the school is run, the way the whole structure of the school functions, relates to the values articulated.

> It was a wonderful challenge and we went right to it. We spent six months or so with questionnaires to parents, workshops for teachers, questionnaires to children. We tried to find out if we had a consensus of the values and then decided what the Quaker values were. We came up with a set of values of this school and then labeled them Quaker values. The structure of present values was identified, not as new values, but as those already existing.

> So here we were identifying a heritage from a very small, residential school that started in Palestine when the student population was almost one hundred percent Christian. A legacy of hidden Quaker values arose from the original Christian school and was carried by value-bearers within the

school, such as teachers. One of the things about this school is how long teachers stay. You could say there is a twenty percent rapid turnover of staff, but really eighty percent of the staff are long-term, serving members of the school who carry the values from one generation to the next — students becoming teachers. We still have a considerable number of staff whose personal history starts as students in the school and now continues as teachers or staff. These hidden values that were carried from one generation to the next are now articulated as part of the heritage of Friends Schools.

The next step then is how do you integrate all these values? The best way was to look at professional development and realize that our teachers needed training. The attitudes in classrooms and in the school didn't always match the values that were articulated. The way that is changed is to go right to the teachers' professional roots and try to give them an understanding of what professionalism as a teacher is. So we decided to do an independent program of professional development which would be internally validated by pay increments if they completed the program successfully. One of the classes would be Quaker ethics.

This process was similar to one that any school wanting a value-driven curriculum would take. But it still didn't directly address the specific Quaker faith issues that are the foundation of what Friends believe are Quaker values. And Colin was well aware as he stated, "I'm still not answering your question, because the basic issue is about faith. Quaker values don't hang in the air but are really faith issues. And then there are complications around that—you have the values of Islam, values of Christianity, and the values of Quakerism."

The faith question in a community that has a strong heritage of both Christianity and Islam is how to balance Christian evangelism and tolerance, and where are the boundaries between them? Colin said, "There is the whole legality of conversion from one faith to another, and it is indeed illegal, and the whole structure of this community being set up so that you are born a Christian and have a Christian education, not an Islamic education; and if you are a Muslim born to a Muslim family, you are required to have an Islamic education. The society is deliberately divided to avoid competition and keep the community separate to avoid conflict."

Colin continued, "So how does a Quaker school with a particular faith relationship come into this kind of milieu—a Christian school in a Muslim community? How does the whole business of the living expression of faith find its place in a school like this? It can only be found in the living faith of people, of teachers who are willing to talk about it without getting to the place where they are bashing people into the Kingdom—it's about sharing. And how do you do that when you have so few Quakers on staff? And, in places, not any Quakers?"

Value-bearers Pass on Quaker Values

Colin identified the importance of "value-bearers within the school, such as teachers." Many teachers through the years have kept alive the Quaker values and passed them on. One such teacher is Donn Hutchison, who has worked under ten of the twenty principals at the Friends Boys School.

Donn recounted,

> There's a picture in the hall in the boys school of the twenty principals; I worked under the last ten

of them and the other ten I know stories about because my mother-in-law and my father-in-law were always involved in the school. One was Moses Bailey [FBS principal 1919-21] and my mother-in-law credits him with having made my father-in-law very westernized. My father-in law loved Moses Bailey.

Moses Bailey was, I suppose, very conservative ... my father-in-law still wore the native dress at the time and spoke in the native dialect. Moses Bailey told him he was a bright boy, but he would never advance if he continued to wear peasant garb, and speak the peasant dialect. And so he came home and he refused to wear the peasant garb any longer; he wore a suit. And he refused to speak the village dialect; he spoke the American Arabic, the city Arabic that the people spoke. I think it always made him a little separate from the rest of the family.

They used to go for long walks to Jericho and all over. And he kind of worshiped the ground Moses Bailey walked on. I think for him, with a peasant background, having an interest shown by this man coming out of the West was a very enlightening thing for him. Because my father-in-law was very, very bright, spoke six or seven languages, and was a doctor, I think he got caught in this world between east and west. I think it was a hard thing for him to bridge at times.

Donn came to Ramallah Friends Schools as a teacher when he was twenty years old and has stayed ever since. He married a Palestinian, and raised several children who now live in the United States. Donn is a widower. Photos of earlier life at the Friends

Schools and in Ramallah, as well as brightly colored paintings and traditional handiwork fill his walls. It is a warm and welcoming spot on the top of the hill overlooking Ramallah.

Donn's impact on the students at the boys school has been profound, as alumni after alumni reported some story or comment about him. Students learned the value of honesty and compassion from watching his daily walk; they were inspired to think more creatively and to challenge base explanations.

"One teacher who had an influence on me is Ustaz Donn Hutchison," wrote Ayed O. Ayed, a 2005 graduate studying medicine in Amman, Jordan. "From him I learned to look at things in a simple way, to give and expect nothing in return, to forgive those who hurt us, to be kind to others, and a lot more. He's much of a stickler when it comes to rules and regulations, but it made me realize that abiding by the law is the key to an orderly and easier life."

"Mr. Donn Hutchinson, without a doubt, made it possible for me to explore different ideas, different ways of writing and presentation," wrote Mona Hasan, 1998 graduate and copywriter in Durham, North Carolina. "Today I have received accolades for my public speaking thanks to his speech classes. And when I think about the freedom of writing he gave us in his composition classes, it makes me realize how much he really did influence me as a writer today."

Another of these value-bearers is Samir Hishmeh, a distant relative of Jacob Hishmeh who helped found Hope School in 1869. Samir had stories to tell about the difficulty Jacob had convincing parents to allow their daughters to have an education. Sabha Hishmeh, Jacob's niece, was one of the first students and became one of the first teachers to arise from the student body. The family connection to Ramallah Friends Schools is strong for Samir and his family.

Samir is a 1962 graduate who taught at the boys school for thirty-five years before retiring. He taught for ten years before moving into administration as dean of students. He was heavily involved with teaching and developing the ethics program during those years.

He is now president of the Orthodox Club, a place for children, youth, and community to gather.

Throughout Samir's long history with Ramallah Friends Schools, he stressed the "need to concentrate on Quaker values" and he remains committed to its future. His hope for the schools future is built on its strong past. "Friends Schools don't need to be ashamed of being Christian schools," he stated, they need to "model Christian values. When the administration has the Quaker values, they reflect the values because they are grounded in faith. FUM needs to work with the administration to make clear that the running of the school is on Quaker values despite all the changes in staff. When a teacher is appointed, they need to look at their values and make sure they match those of the school."

In the 1970s, "FUM sent many volunteers who were always ready to help, to forgive, and to feel for others," Samir said. These qualities were viewed as relating to one's faith. As Samir talked, it was easy to see how much he loved his students and cared about the future of the Friends Schools. "My greatest happiness," he said, "was when I would reach someone with forgiveness. I was successful when I built good relations with the students, and they would trust me, and I would be there to help them." He is now funneling his compassion and experience into the children and youth at the Orthodox Club. Working with young people is his joy.

This continuity of passing on Quaker values—through students becoming teachers and teachers remaining for many years—is a strength of the Friends Schools which is manifest in people like Donn and Samir, and many others.

Quaker Values Impact Adult Life

Stressing Quaker values has led to many prominently placed alumni in leadership positions. Joyce Ajlouny graduated in 1983 and since 2004 has been serving as the Friends Schools director. She has the experience of being a student and now a school administrator. As a Palestinian Quaker, she is strongly committed to strengthening the Quaker values in the school system.

"I remember when I was asked about my vision for the school when I first got here," she stated, "and I said one thing—if I continue hearing from alumni that this school has made a profound impact in their lives, I think the mission is accomplished. And this is what we want to continue doing, influencing people's lives in that positive way so they would understand what nonviolence means, what peace and justice means. We are trying harder in the school, because throughout the years, I think we saw some ups and downs in terms of specific effort going towards working on values. I don't think in any year at any given time the school let go of the [Quaker] values.

"The values are intrinsic but sometimes throughout the years we have seen some concerted effort to work more on the values. Since I have been here, I have been trying to do that with the ethics program and design courses that specifically look at our values, like the comparative religion course or conflict resolution course or a Quakerism course."

In the 2006-07 school year, two specific Quaker classes were added to the ethics curriculum — *Quaker Faith and Practice* for eleventh graders and *Quaker History* for eighth graders. *Quaker Faith and Practice* helps students articulate specific Quaker values and what they mean to them personally.

The *Quaker History* class focuses on early Quaker history, the history of Friends in the Middle East, and the history of Ramallah Friends Schools. An opportunity to have students share in the education of other students attending Quaker schools world-wide was deliberately built into the curriculum.

Joyce said,

> When I am talking to my eighth grade students about the importance of giving and that giving is more meaningful than receiving. I am giving them an opportunity--like the project of giving to Turkana [Africa] and Amari [the Friends preschool in the Amari refugee camp near the Friends Boys School]. You need to feel what it feels like to give. So I know they will grow up with this value.

> I can see they [RFS graduates] carry those values with them and no doubt if someone is the head of an organization, or working in the government, these values are going to translate and have a trickle-down effect to colleagues, staff, children, etc. So many of the alumni who I see or come to visit me tell me time and time again that if it weren't for the experiences at the Friends Schools, they wouldn't be who they are today or where they are today.

> And I would like to focus on the "who" they are today because the "who" is what is really inside you. And who you are as a person, and what you believe in, and your value system. And they are giving credit to the Friends Schools. And this is something that makes us very proud and I know there are very few schools in the world that could claim such impact. But we hear it over and over again.

A lot of our graduates are prominently placed decision makers, etc. But it is not only the education
that we provide, it is also the Quaker values we provide, that we try to instill in our students. When
they move on and become the decision makers and
influential people, our hope is that they take these
values with them in their adult life and their professional lives. If our theory holds that they actually
take these values with them, then we can say that
the school has had an impact in terms of its Quaker
values on so many aspects of life in Palestine.

Chapter 3
Equality

When Hope School first opened in 1869, the Quaker testimony of equality was put into action. With the opening of Friends Girls Boarding School in 1889, another step toward equality was taken.

Then in 1901, equality took a new turn as parents requested a school for their sons as good as the one they were sending their daughters to attend. Ground was purchased and building began. The first class of boys graduated in 1906.

Equality took several other forms over the years. Though it began as a school for Christian students, Muslim students were not turned away, and now constitute the majority of students (see Chapter Four). The Friends Schools also became the first Palestinian co-educational schools in the 1960s, allowing boys and girls to study in the same classrooms with the same teachers. In addition, they now have the only mainstreamed special needs program in Palestine.

Since their founding, Friends Schools have been at the forefront of demonstrating the testimony of equality in concrete forms, between genders, between faiths, and between abilities.

Pioneering Women's Education

Friends Girls School is a pioneer in women's education for Palestine and the region. When the Girls Schools first opened, they provided opportunities for Christian girls to break out of traditional patterns and have a different kind of future.

Mahmoud Arma, 1979 graduate and current head of FBS, said,

> I think that the school has played a major role in that it was the first school to provide an education for girls. At that time a girl going to school was very weird, or very strange. We have come a long way in that now we have more girls than boys going to school. The percentage of girls in both schools is higher.

> But I will say it is still difficult for many families to grasp the idea to provide further education for girls. Or let me say if a family has a boy and a girl, and they can only send one of them to college, it will be the boy. This is still the case for many families in the villages. When families in our schools face financial problems, and they have a girl and a boy in the school, they would choose to keep the boy in the school. Now we have a higher percentage of boys over girls—about forty-five percent girls and fifty-five percent boys. Although the percentages are very close, it still tells you something about the preference to educate the boys.

> The culture the school is trying to promote, that boys and girls are equal, you can see how this is re-

flected in the everyday life of the students. You can see how the boys and girls are changing each other in a totally equal way, but this is not the case in society. And many of the families are sending their children to the school just for that reason, because they believe the school promotes equality in both genders, promotes open-mindedness. You keep hearing from families that say this is the most important factor for us as a family.

One student who was impacted by the example of both gender and economic equality was Huda Qubein Kraske, a 1960 graduate who lives in Washington, D.C. She related this story about her years at Friends Girls School and how important equality was for her, a poor girl:

When the FGS principal Annice Carter heard that my mother had marital difficulties, she offered me a scholarship, without which I would not have been able to attend the FGS. The only way I could level the playing field with all the rich girls around me was to excel in my studies, and this led to my being the valedictorian at my graduation in 1960.

Miss Carter's kindness and words of encouragement helped me plough on. She was also good enough to give me some of the clothing packages that were sent by kindly hearts in the United States, which I desperately needed.

One evening, when Miss Carter began a music appreciation get-together for upper school boarding students, she noticed that I was absolutely thrilled by what I heard. The next day, she called me in and said that she would pay for one year of piano lessons which I enjoyed tremendously. That, of course, was the only music teaching I ever had, but I can still read notes. I do not know if the funds came out of her own pocket or out of some school fund. I will never forget what she and the FGS did for me.

After graduation, Huda Qubein Kraske traveled to the U.S. to attend the American University in Washington, D.C., where she majored in economics.

The equality testimony is about opening doors. "It opens doors for girls and boys, especially for girls," states Diana Abdul Nour, principal of FGS. "I think we are the only school here [in Palestine] that stresses taking fifty percent girls and fifty percent boys—we even take fifty-three percent girls because we know that through time we will lose one or two girls. If we did like the other schools, first come-first served, we would have only about ten percent girls. Priority is given to girls and that makes some parents who have males unhappy. We have to keep a balance. It gives hope and this is the most important—hope for parents, hope for children. You can't imagine how many more children want to come to this school."

Cultural Impact

Several people stated in their interviews that when the girls schools were started they provided new opportunities for Christian girls, but now, in this day and age when there are more Muslims than Christians in the school, it is providing those same opportunities and the same transformation within the Muslim culture that it did within the Christian culture over 100 years ago.

The girls who previously attended the Friends Girls School were "taught Friends testimonies like equality," stated Joy Totah-Hilden of Berkeley, California, daughter of former boys school principal, Kahlil Totah. "Equality lifted up and empowered the Christian girls who were going to the school in the early days. Both of the Ramallah Friends Schools are now doing the same thing for the Muslim girls who are attending, empowering them to have a future as they want."

People on the streets know the schools provide quality education for both boys and girls, and generally see this as a good thing. The parents who send their daughters to RFS see education as a way to provide hope for their futures, and to help them become leaders in Palestinian life.

"RFS offers hope," stated Holly Dhynes, FUM field staff from 1997-2000. "It represents the place where Palestinian society wants to be, a place of quality education, equality for women, and peace."

Because the school has stood for equality since 1869, the impact on the role of women has been profound and has been a countercultural challenge within the community. Men and women receive an equal education, providing equal opportunities for both genders to internalize the same career values and expectations.

Joyce Ajlouny, 1983 graduate and current RFS director, said,

> The fact that I haven't really thought much about it is a good thing. It is because in this school it exemplifies gender equity and what it means. There are no differences in our hiring procedures, our admission procedures (one of our policies for admission is a point system and girls get an extra point so we have a preference for girls). And that is be-

cause our culture does not do so. Even if we do a fifty-fifty in kindergarten, by the time they are in seventh or eighth grade, there are more boys than girls. We want to admit more girls in the beginning because they will start dwindling. [If a family has] three kids and two boys and a girl, and they can't afford to send all three to RFS, they will choose to send the boys here and not the girl. So they will send her out to another school. We also have some preferential treatment for girls when it comes to our financial aid office. Sometimes we have supporters who come and say we want to support girls because we know they are less fortunate. So we have more girls receiving child sponsorships, for example, than boys.

I am a big gender equity advocate. What I find here is that I don't need to say a thing; it's happening. When we were selecting students to go to the Model United Nations in Qatar, I didn't have to say, "Make sure we have enough girls." No, on the contrary, of the eighteen who went, twelve were girls. I think this is lovely.

This culture does try to suppress women, put women down, or say, "You know nothing." We teach girls to be assertive and to speak up and not shy away because this is what their culture expects them to do—give a chance for the man to speak, listen to the man, agree with the man, but we are saying, "No, no, no … you have an equal say," and they go out and they prove themselves. And they are assertive in their approaches and their relationships.

Statistically proven, all but one or two students from each graduating class go on to college, either abroad or in Palestine. This means that most girls are going on to college and working on higher education degrees. Joyce said, "Our women are very ambitious. Many finish their bachelor's and say it's time for the master's, and then the doctorate. They want a career; they don't want to just get married and have kids. They see that life offers more for them, and they want to take advantage of it all."

Obtaining a degree offers women a wider perspective and greater opportunities for the future. Gender equality raises women to be fully competent. The modern role for many women in Palestine has been transformed by the enduring presence of the Ramallah Friends Schools and the value of equality that it models.

Social Impact

"Another thing that gives hope is the social factor," stated Mahmoud Arma, 1979 graduate and principal of FBS. "I believe that the school provides a very healthy social environment for the students, when we are talking about gender inclusion. This is one of very few schools [in Palestine] that is co-educational. This also gives social hope."

The testimony of equality led to a new model of RFS education—changing from separate schools for boys and girls into a co-educational model. Mazen Karam, a 1971 graduate, described the process he experienced as the transition was made at the schools. His class of 1971 had thirteen boys and five girls. During his high school years, they began working toward co-education, rather than just having some girls attend some classes at the FBS. "We were the guinea pigs. They tried co-ed classes in my eighth grade; it didn't work. In eleventh grade, boys took Arabic at FGS and girls came to the FBS for sixth to eighth periods. When I graduated it was fully co-educational, but it took four years to work it out."

More recently, "the school has been pioneering in girls sports," stated Director Joyce Ajlouny. "We started the first girls soccer team, and then we encouraged other schools to establish girls soccer teams, and now there is a tournament. We take credit for that because we really pioneered for our community to look at opportunities for girls in sports."

Attending a co-educational school and participating in sports and other activities "also gives another dimension to the woman who has a well-rounded personality, a woman who is not afraid or hesitant in saying what she thinks," stated Mahmoud Arma. "We get feedback from organizations where our students have applied to work. Whether it is in the interviews or the way they present themselves, people see that there is something different about a Friends Schools graduate."

Mahmoud continued, "The girls who are going to the school are getting their education, and are proving to be able to continue their college education, which affects the society by setting examples of girls who can be educated and be leaders in their fields. And we now have many, many such women. In fact, many organizations in the culture that are successful are led by women, many of whom are graduates of the school."

Special Needs Program

Taking the equality testimony seriously caused RFS to move in a new direction. Social equality was not just between the genders, but also between abilities. Since 1994, RFS has offered hope to children and parents whose children have special needs.

"It makes me happy because thirteen years ago I started the special needs program because I believed in it," stated Diana Abdul Nour, principal of FGS. "I believe that they have rights."

The process took a tenacious person to move it forward. The first proposal for inclusive mainstreaming of special needs students was not accepted. Then a one-year pilot project was begun to serve the three percent of the population who had special needs. Funds were raised and a teacher from Amman, Jordan, was hired. The pilot project was evaluated after one year by staff and parents and placed in the annual budget as a regular program with one teacher and volunteers.

As a result of strategic planning, the program was extended to the boys school so that students who began at the elementary level could continue in the mainstreaming program through high school. RFS offers the only mainstreaming program for special needs students in Palestine; all other schools have separate classrooms or even special schools for these students. "For parents who were desperate and hopeless," stated Diana Abdul Nour, "we gave them a ray of light when the doors were opened."

For some parents, this ray of light is what helps to keep them in Palestine, rather than emigrating. "RFS provides hope for families with children with special needs. The children have nowhere else to go that would include them in the mainstream educational system. This hits home for me," states Joyce Ajlouny. "Even way before I was involved with this school in the capacity of director, I always said that if not for the Friends Schools we would be in the United States because there is nothing in town available for my son Nadar. So this is an important aspect of giving hope to these kids and these families."

Quaker values are not just a curriculum; they are a way of life. Several RFS students are now working with children with special needs. One student is Maria Lisa Araj Mufareh, a 1997 graduate living in Baltimore, Maryland. She wrote, "I remember being extremely afraid of attending Friends [Schools] because I just came from the States not knowing what to expect. However, I was welcomed by so many nice people and the staff was amazing. I always thought, 'Wow, they're so smart, one day I want to be a teacher and give back to the community.' And now I am! I teach at a school for learning disabled children called the Baltimore Lab School (fifth grade)."

Chapter 4
Tolerance and Respect

Most students weren't able to distinguish between Muslim and Christian students when they attended RFS. This does not mean that Friends have failed in their mission at the Schools, but that a deep understanding of tolerance and respect has taken root.

Students at RFS focus on the character of their friends rather than their religious holdings. Not everything has rigid boundaries for these students, which makes them more tolerant and respectful towards one another.

"And the fact is," states Mahmoud Arma, 1979 graduate and head of FBS, "that our students come from different faiths and often graduate without even knowing this person is Muslim and this person is Christian. This means that the school is affecting the open-mindedness and acceptance of other faiths, and helps students live together in a very humane group."

"Religious faith is not a new concept in this region of the world," Mahmoud continued. "You don't have people who are without religion. There are areas in the world where people haven't heard yet about religion, but this is a totally different situation. For instance, people are born into a family who, for hundreds of years, has been Catholic or Muslim or another. It is possible somebody could be converted, but even if someone is convinced in a new faith, there are many social obstacles to change that. So I would say this is impossible to change one's religion because of [history and heritage]. But we certainly have many people who believe in the principles of Quakers which, I think, in the long run serves the cause of Quakerism in a very good way."

Value Bearers

Tolerance is a Quaker value that has been passed down by value bearers in the schools.

Farid Tabri was one such value bearer. He was a beloved teacher and administrator at the boys school for almost fifty years before retiring (1919-68). He taught Arabic and later became dean. He also led chapel, reading one day from the Bible and the next day from the Koran. A Christian, he studied Arabic in Egypt with a great Muslim religious teacher, went to college in Germany where he met his wife, and spent his life dedicated to the Friends Schools when they were boarding schools. His two daughters are also retired from FBS—Salwa Tabri was a music teacher and Fadwa Tabri was a librarian.

As a dedicated Christian, Farid had a profound impact on many students. Issa Cook, a 1954 graduate who now lives in Houston, Texas, talked lovingly about Farid and how he modeled tolerance and respect for the students. "Because of the influence of Farid Tabri," Issa said, "I memorized the Koran. Both of us were Christians, but we learned the Koran."

Issa married another Friends Schools graduate and they have raised their children with Quaker principles. The values taught at RFS had a profound impact on their lives, and lives on in their children.

"RFS certainly did shape our characters, especially my wife and I," Issa continued. "It has influenced all of our lives. We are connected through the school and I talk to other grads at least once a week. It is like a family. We continue to maintain connections with our classmates. It was like a fraternity, a family. Everyone I know went to that school."

Ahmed Kasem Abu Kafieh, a 1952 graduate and retired chemical engineer who lives north of Ramallah, also fondly remembers: "As a boarding student, it was the most memorable time of my life. I was mostly influenced by my Arabic (Mr. Tabri) and math (Mr. Salem) teachers. The happiest occasion was the annual Suke-Okaz contest in Arabic poetry which signaled the end of the school year. Other memorable events and places were the ringing of the bell rituals, the study hall hours, the Sunday dormitory inspections by Mr. Jones and the prefect on duty, the dining room table quotations, the morning chapels, and the singing of hymns prior to beginning of classes. As one of the five student prefects (three boarding and two day), the duties taught me order, promptness, camaraderie, and responsibility. We were always striving for achievement and the pursuit of excellence."

Michael Karam, a 1957 graduate, is a medical doctor living in Raleigh, North Carolina. As a senior at FBS, he was chosen to represent the Jordanian Kingdom at the Chicago Herald Tribune essay contest. He and his finished essay traveled to the United States to accept the award representing his country. The essay was sent to President Eisenhower, who wrote a letter of congratulations back to Michael.

"We were taught about all religions," Michael stated in a phone interview. "Christians and Muslims all were studying the same things. It taught us tolerance and how to accept differences in people. It is carried forth into life. I wish more schools were like Friends Schools in the Middle East."

Religion is Foundational

"One of the things I liked the most was chapel. We would start every day with hymns," stated Hala Karam, a 1971 graduate who lives in Ramallah.

61

Samir Hishmeh was responsible for the chapel program during the thirty-five years he spent at FBS and followed the traditions of previous leaders. "Chapel is the best way to start one's day!" he stated. Chapel started with a moment of silence, and was followed by about five minutes to evaluate the day, concentrating on positive ways to contribute while drawing attention to negative ways students were behaving. Different classes took turns leading chapel, giving everyone an opportunity to speak before the group. In the 1960s and 1970s, they had chapel three times a week, but now it is once a week on Mondays.

The importance of the chapel program goes beyond religion. Kathy South, who worked as a college counselor, helping students with their essays and paperwork for college, stated, "One of the things the students said was important to them was that they were able to participate in the weekly chapel program. It helped them to show leadership, gave them confidence, and developed speaking skills."

"The thing I liked the most was the twenty minutes before we started classes," stated Samia Ajlouny, a 1969 graduate living in California. "Some days in our classroom—and I think three days [in] Swift Hall, [we went] for chapel and praying. We had a tradition that the twelfth grade students lead and take turns to present. It was fortunate for us to be able to stand up and speak, but it was scary at the beginning. And we would sing hymns. Actually one time I heard my favorite hymn on the radio and I ordered the cassette. It was 'Onward, Christian Soldiers,' and I would sing it in my heart and head."

When asked if the religious training she received at RFS was important, Samia replied, "Yes, very important. As a Christian growing up in a Muslim country, going to a Christian school was great because I studied the principles of Christianity: love, care, peace. I took an ethics class where they taught us the principles of every religion—Buddhism, Confucianism, Christianity, Islam — so we were open, not only to one religion and that's it. It was so important to have the teaching of these ethics classes and even over thirty years later, they were the most important of my time there."

Other alumni reported the importance of the ethics curriculum in their lives today. A 1976 graduate, Iman Odeh-Yabroudi, who lives in Dubai, United Arab Emirates, wrote, "The teacher and subject that greatly influenced me was Miss Boutros, who taught a subject called ethics. Her primary goal was to teach ethics as a way of life, not pertaining to a certain religion or creed. I am proud to have learned from her impartiality and non-prejudice. I always do my best to be fair and accommodating of any religion and race and try to teach my children these values. It might sound cheesy, but it's true."

Cheesy or not, the equal readings from the Bible and Koran in chapel, and the integration of ethics within the curriculum, influenced many students. Reema Ali, a 1976 graduate, attended college in England, then moved to the United States. She is presently practicing law in Falls Church, Virginia. She wrote, "I think tolerance of other religions was a big thing that influenced me. I am a Muslim and never felt an outsider or a minority in that school."

Another graduate who lives in the United States is Ghada Dahir, class of 1989. She wrote, "I came to Charlotte, North Carolina, and stayed. I graduated with an English degree and minored in religious studies, which I can also say was a decision I made because of the great relationships Christians and Muslims had back at FGS."

Religion has always been foundational to RFS, expressed through chapel, religion classes, and ethics. But in 1989, the intentional teaching of Islam as well as Christianity became mandatory.

Diana Abdul Nour, principal of FGS, said,

> FGS is a Quaker school, so when I interview families I ask them, "Why do you choose the Friends Schools? Do you know that it is a Christian Quaker school? And that we teach Quaker values?" I stress the philosophy of the school and what are the principles of the school. Sometimes people think the Friends Schools are not tied to a church like other Christian schools; sometimes they say they want to come to the school because it is not religious. I don't want them to think this is a secular school. This school belongs to a Christian church and we teach according to their philosophies.
>
> Before 1989 we did not teach religion. After the Intifada, some parents complained to the Minister of Education that they wanted their children to learn Islam. So the Minister of Education forced us to, so we had no choice but to teach it.
>
> When the children start separating for religion in the first grade, [Christians taught in one classroom and Muslims in another,] they usually find it hard. So, for the first month we don't separate them and the Christian religion teacher and the Muslim religion teacher teach together. They talk about things [the two religions have] in common, because this is the first time that children hear the word religion. The two teachers prepare them for the separation so it is not something strange for the children and they are not surprised by it.

I had to do this because when I started here the first year my daughter was in first grade. She refused to go with the Christians because she wanted to be with her friend. She asked why her friend had to go to a different class and what is the difference between a Muslim and a Christian? So I started thinking of a way to prepare them. I discussed it with the teachers and now we have a time to prepare the students.

"I remember my first Islam Religion teacher, Mrs. Lina Hamoudah," wrote Besan Al-Omary, a 2001 graduate from Ramallah. "She taught religion with such a kind heart, unlike many teachers who attempt to scare us into religion."

"I had a great time growing up at the Friends Boys School as a young girl," stated Ahlam Basem Allan, a 2001 graduate who lives in Grand Rapids, Michigan. "I found it very different from going to school in the United States. The sheer fact of being around people that are very close to you either in religion or culture is very refreshing and an enlightening experience. I always had to be conscious of myself growing up in the States because my culture and religion entail different things than those of the Americans. I made many, many friends of which I still keep in touch with. I felt that I was really a part of a society, rather than having to be picked out of one."

"I had a very strong education that really has benefited me now, while I attend college as well as raise a young family. I learned to function under pressure and to try to maximize my output with much efficiency. I learned to be a good friend and felt compassion for those who are really in need."

Friends' influence is both personal and communal. Holly Dhynes, FUM field staff from 1997-2000, claimed that there were two ways Quakers are influential at RFS. First, through the teaching of Quaker values and the reputation in the community of producing individuals who evidence those values. And secondly, through the "ethics courses which every student takes and learns."

Character Development

The integration of Quaker values and ethics in all courses produces students who develop character in ways different from the prevailing culture. A 2005 graduate, Ayed O. Ayed, is studying medicine in Amman, Jordan. He was full of zeal for Friends Schools and the person he became because of his time there.

> My ethics classes taught me the character of human rights. The ethics classes were grounded in Quaker values. But ethics was integrated in all classes which made them more successful, rather than if they were just one subject. They were interdisciplinary, utilizing common themes and ideas. The classes I took were valuable for me and helps me pull things together and shows me connections I had not been exposed to before. My education at the RFS helps me be a more well-rounded individual.
>
> I developed many of the beliefs and ideals I hold today during my years at RFS. I believe that we should be tolerant of other people, regardless of their beliefs and other ways in which they may differ from us. I strongly agree with peace and negotiation as tools to solve our problems rather than the use of brute force. Further, my appreciation of science and research, love for knowledge, and pursuit of excellence were all influenced by the Friends Schools. Notably, my understanding of democracy, justice, creativity, and service were influenced by RFS, too.

Many students say that they would not be where they are today if it weren't for the education provided by RFS. They refer not only to the education they received, but also to the character development which occurred within them during their years at the Friends Schools.

Rana Bahu Toubassi, a 1988 graduate living in Ramallah, is a lawyer working on a European Union project for empowering the Palestinian Judiciary. Her character is important to the work she does and makes her who she is today.

"In general," she stated, "being a student at the FGS had a great impact on my life in regards to developing the personality, preserving good relationships and developing good communication within the community, and in developing tolerance and patience to work hard for what I want to achieve in life."

Several others stated it more simply. "The years I spent at the Friends Schools were great and left a great impact on my life and where I am now," wrote Jacob Zarou, a 1980 graduate who lives on Long Island, New York.

"I will just sum it up with a few words," wrote Ramzi A. Nuri, a 1977 graduate living in Dubai, United Arab Emirates. "Friends Schools is the backbone of our success in life, whether it is economic success, monetary success, educational, etc., is irrelevant."

Samia Ajlouny, a 1969 graduate, credits RFS for developing honesty within her. "Honesty was always with me," she said. "Cheating was the worst thing to happen. It was unacceptable. And we were punished really heavily with that. … This honesty is even at work now. Even my boss one time said, 'Samia, you are too honest.' The impact of the school is seen in my work. During my review he said, 'Since you came here, everything is calm and there is more teamwork. You have helped people to forget their differences and work together.' And I said to them, 'Remember, I spent fourteen years with the Quakers.'"

Personalities are shaped and character is developed within those who attend RFS. Celine Khoury graduated in 2005, and is studying interior design in Lebanon. She stated, "The academic standards of the school, along with its activities, programs, traditions, and the atmosphere in general, all allowed us to be distinguished in the society, as well as other societies. In other words, it's really true when they say that Friends Schools students have especially strong personalities. I don't know what exactly is responsible for that, but I know it's true. It's just a Friends School 'secret.'"

Tamara Asad, a 2000 graduate of the Friends Schools who went on to graduate from Guilford College in 2004, valued the Quaker principles of human equality, and the respect for the worth and dignity of each human being, she learned at RFS. While a student at Guilford, she was the babysitter for an Israeli couple living in Greensboro, the husband of which had been a member of the Israeli Defense Forces unit that occupied her neighborhood in Ramallah.

Yacoub Sa'ad, a 2004 graduate of the Friends Schools and 2008 graduate of Guilford, brought a message to College Meeting for Worship during his senior year. He said, "I began to see a totally different role of faith in someone's life; it is more personal; it is reflected through one's lifestyle. I admired the fact that, instead of lecturing the religious values and teaching to have faith, people are actually living through their faith. Soon, there was an urge inside of me to make a difference in my life, and in the lives of those around me."

Many alumni feel the pull back to Ramallah Friends Schools and return to visit later in life. Eman Khaldon Ottallah, a 1999 graduate living in Panama City, Florida, wrote:

> I really, really miss the FBS. The first place I visit when I come to Palestine is always the FBS. It's always very emotional when I go back, and every

teacher has had such a positive influence on my life. Other than Allah and my family, I would say that where I am today is largely in part to my experience at the FBS. ... But, in reality, [anyone] who can read and write has the potential to have a great education ... the one thing that differs between those who make it and those who don't is the drive. And the FBS (like the sign above the main entrance door that states that the pen is stronger than the sword) gave us the drive to take advantage of getting the best education we could. The students are incredible. I have yet to meet people that even come close to FBS grads in terms of sincerity and character.

For others, the pull brings them back so their children can experience the same values in their education. One such family involves Mazen Karam, a 1971 graduate who followed in his father's footsteps; he and his five brothers and one sister all graduated from RFS. After spending eight years in the United States, Mazen and his wife and children packed up and moved back to Ramallah so his children could have the quality of education and character development he received from RFS. He currently serves on the Ramallah Friends Schools Board of Trustees and enthusiastically spoke about "his" school:

The Friends School allowed me a smooth transition into college and a chance to excel because of the good education and sports program. There were no taboos to carry forward to future years. There was always encouragement to excel, research, and improvise. The relation between students and most teachers was always that of friendship.

I carried forward those beliefs and practices into my college life and work environment, which was instrumental in my career development to executive levels. Similarly in my community relations, the close friendships with fellow classmates and teachers helped me establish more friends while keeping my old ones.

The special relation between the school and its former students helped me stay close to the school and made me and my wife move back to Ramallah so that our children could attend the same school that we and my father attended. I am proud to have one graduate in 2003 and two more to graduate in 2008 and 2009. I can feel that while many things have changed at the school, the education my children are getting is similar to what I got.

For others who don't return to Ramallah, recognizing the exceptional education they received provides hope that the values they learned can be passed on to their children wherever they are. Majeed G. Makhlouf, a 1994 graduate and Cleveland, Ohio, attorney wrote, "Without having had the privilege of attending RFS, I would not be where I am today. Now having two daughters of my own and going through the process of selecting a school for them, I am more than ever appreciative of the experiences that I gained at RFS."

The experiences at RFS, whether as boarding students or as day students, have been internalized and continue to carry a profound influence on the lives of alumni. Akel Biltaji, a 1959 graduate living in Amman, Jordan, wrote for the Friends Schools newsletter about his experiences:

It has been over forty-five years since I left the Friends Boys School (FBS) in Ramallah. I still carry around the memories of the good old days, the beautiful people, the great learning, and the unique campus where I was privileged to spend some of the most exciting years of my life. It was at the FBS when I started to learn how to live in a larger family, how to share, and, most importantly, how to accept and respect the other. It was the grounds where I found peace within myself and with others. It was at a time when teachers stood as mentors and led the student body to an active role in the community. Fixing my bed, cleaning the dormitory, waiting at the dining room, maintaining the appearance and the grounds of the campus, singing in the choir, playing all kinds of sports, leading the Lions (soccer), retaining the position of the head prefect of the school in 1958 after it was abolished in 1941, standing on the stage and extemporaneously talking about the subject of the day—all of that made me what I am today. I would not have been the successful teacher, the leading public relations man, the high ranking airline executive, the minister of tourism and antiquities, the founding chief commissioner for the Aqaba Special Economic Zone, the advisor to H.M. King Abdullah II, and now a member of the Jordanian Senate, had all that not been for the values and ethics of the Friends Society, the teaching and discipline of the school, and the commitment and quality of the staff. The diversified and great student body was an important element in my life which has helped me to be sociable and a team player. The Friends School was more than a school;

it was a way of life that has enabled me and so many others to become community leaders, great academicians, and successful businessmen.

Chapter 5
Intellectual Freedom

Ramallah has undergone many transitions and been under occupation by several different countries. These historical events have had an effect upon Ramallah Friends Schools and the teaching staff. But throughout the numerous changes, the schools have maintained an air of openness and intellectual freedom that is not seen in other schools. Nurturing intellectual freedom has fostered hope in individuals and the community.

"Because the schools have been in the community almost 140 years," Retha McCutchen stated, "it is hard to tell how many ways they have offered hope to the community. But what would Ramallah have been like without the influence and standards set by the Friends Schools? They were often pacesetters and set standards that were later adopted by other schools, as well as being in the forefront of cultural programs in the community." Retha served as director of RFS from 1995-97 and as FUM World Ministries director from 1997-2004 and FUM General Secretary from 1997-2006.

In classes, students have always had the freedom to write about what was happening around them. Issa Cook was the deputy mayor of Ramallah when the Israel Defense Force came into Ramallah and occupied it in 1967. He said that one of his sons wrote an article for a class at Friends Girls School, when he was eight years old, about how the occupation made him feel. Issa stated, "Soldiers came to the school, and read [the article] and wanted to take him to jail. Eight years old! The principal interfered and had him released. This son is now a doctor in Houston."

Throughout the years, this same commitment to teach students to express themselves remains. Reema Ali, a 1976 graduate who is practicing law in Falls Church, Virginia, stated it well, "When one lives under occupation, one loses the right to freedom of expression and all civil liberties. FGS was the oasis where I experienced freedom of expression and my rights as a student. I grew up knowing that not being able to express ones-self freely is not the norm."

Freedom of Expression

John Hishmeh served as college counselor and activities director during his term as FUM Field Staff from 2004-07. He expressed the difference he saw in Ramallah Friends Schools and other schools in the community and Palestine:

> At the Friends Schools you will find a different atmosphere than you will find in any other school around here. That doesn't mean we don't have our set of problems, and some are big problems just like anybody else. But you will find here an openness and a freedom that you won't find in other schools—a freedom of expression. Students feel free to express themselves. Students are encouraged to take initiative on projects they are interested in. We have a very active student council that is involved with the administration, that is involved with teachers, that is involved with the students and doing yearly activities. We have activities every year like the Ju-

nior/Senior Dance, our equivalent of a prom. No other school in this area would have anything like that.

That is the kind of atmosphere we have that is free and is open. The students are free to enjoy themselves and to interact at an open level. They are not restricted by fundamentalist thought or impressions or whatever you want to call it. But what I find particularly special about this campus is the freedom that students experience. They are free to engage with their teachers, free to engage with the administration, free to express themselves. They have chapel and forums — venues to express, to demonstrate, and have awareness discussions. All those elements, I don't know, maybe you would call them democratic principles, but there is a freedom here that doesn't exist in other places.

I personally think one of the best qualities of our school is that students can come here and be free to express themselves and be who they really want to be. And in terms of them growing up and developing their personalities and preparing them for the future, in this place having a school like this is a gem. It's a gem because you just don't find it anywhere else. And it gives our students practice in expressing themselves, practice at having interests and having talents, having passions or hobbies or interests; it gives them opportunities to explore all those things where they wouldn't have them in other places.

The Friends Schools continue to develop critical thinking and nurture openness. Teachers coming from different schools notice the difference immediately. Joyce Ajlouny, a 1983 graduate and current director, describes this phenomenon: "If a teacher comes here from any other school, they say, 'Oh, this is different than what I am used to.' The teacher/student relationship is based on openness, on respect. It is based on the fact that the teacher does not come to the classroom with the attitude, 'I have the only opinion,' or, 'I know everything and you know nothing.' Many of the schools in the U.S. take these things for granted, but this is a different culture. Here students do not speak out, their opinion is suppressed, and this is where this school is being different."

Value Bearers

The relationship between teachers and students has been one of developing relationships. Intellectual freedom cannot just be taught; it must also be modeled by teachers so that students can see the value in action.

Majeed G. Makhlouf, 1984 graduate and an attorney living in Cleveland, Ohio, said:

> Our teachers treated us like friends. We often met with teachers after school. We visited them at their homes, and they visited us at our homes. In fact, both times that I visited Ramallah after I moved to the United States, my top priority was to [see] my teachers and classmates.
>
> Perhaps the primary contribution we gained at RFS was to learn to think. RFS did not simply teach us history. It taught us how to question history and research it. It didn't only teach us chemistry from a textbook. It emphasized the laboratory and research

components of chemistry. These are qualities that you keep for life, even if you forget the specifics of what you learned.

In some ways, we didn't know who Socrates was when we were students at RFS, but his invisible hand was in our classes. This is a skill set that I cherish greatly today as an attorney.

Several teachers were mentioned specifically in the responses from alumni as nurturing this quality of critical thinking. Mona Hasan, a 1998 graduate living in Durham, North Carolina, noted two teachers who helped her grow. "Mr. Peter Kapenga, a former history teacher, was probably one of the most influential teachers any of us ever had, especially when it came to Palestinian history. He was more than a teacher, but a real thought-provoker. Until this day, I think about him when it comes to really opening my mind to a problem and seeking the solution. He was the only one who knew that sometimes there was no right answer, but knowing the problem made all the difference. He made knowledge fun."

Besan Al-Omary, a 2001 graduate, lives in Ramallah and works as a producer/reporter for Al-Jazeera Satellite Channel. He remembers, "Miss Tina Rafidi (English) taught us Shakespeare in an awesome way. I am still proud to say I understand his sonnets and enjoy them dearly. There are so many other teachers who are really amazing."

"Our class was the first to try out for International Baccalaureate (IB)," he recalls, "and we couldn't have passed it without our teachers who spent day and night for two years giving us their best. Truly, each and every teacher deserves our thanks and hopes, as they helped us become who we are today."

Each teacher is a gem, which transforms Friends Schools into a shining jewel of Palestine. Their dedication, especially during the Intifadas and during the addition of the International Baccalaureate (IB) degree, has impacted the students and the community.

"Because I grew up in the States and moved to Ramallah when I was fourteen," said Maria Lisa Araj Mufareh, a 1997 graduate living in Baltimore, Maryland, "and with the education I received at Friends, I believe it helped me get into one of the best universities in the States. I am a strong and independent individual today and I believe Friends had a lot to do with it."

Amra Amra, a 2003 graduate attending Birzeit University and majoring in finance, contends, "After attending the Friends, I became more social and appreciative. I now am more thankful and connected with humanity. The things I used to take for granted I now cherish. I feel sorry for the millions of people who are blinded by their ignorance. This opportunity truly broadened my horizons and allowed me to be more connected to my community and heritage."

Ayed O. Ayed, a 2005 graduate studying medicine in Amman, Jordan, was born in Saudi Arabia and moved to Ramallah when he was six years old. He began attending RFS in the third grade. He stated, "My view of the world sprouted from RFS and my exposure to a wider worldview. From the Friends Schools, I received strongly convicted ideas. It helped me to be exposed to other values and saved me from the tunnel vision many Palestinians have of 'kill and conquer.' As long as people carry ideas like I do, there is hope."

Hope

"Our Quaker concern," stated Colin South, 2000-04 RFS director, "is to grow people who can make their own decisions about their own lives. Mahmoud Arma, head of FBS, has been very concerned about student participation and involving students in democracy and decision making."

Mahmoud attended Friends Schools himself and graduated in 1979. After attending college in Germany, he received a degree in physics. He returned to Ramallah and taught physics and math at FBS for ten years before moving into administration in 1996. His two children also attend the Friends Schools. He has a wide perspective on the Friends Schools, as an alumnus, as a teacher, as an administrator, and as a parent. He shared three ways he sees that Friends Schools provide hope:

> In my opinion, the first and most obvious way is the academic perspective. It is well known that the school is very competitive in academics, even at international levels. We have one of the most demanding international programs with the International Baccalaureate (IB) program. All through its history, the school has provided a very demanding, competitive academic program. So I believe that having such a school in this country gives people hope that students can get a good education in this school and be competitive worldwide.
>
> Students who get their education at this school and get such academic preparation for their life can also provide hope to help this country solve its multifaceted problems.
>
> The school has always been at the front of experimenting with and enhancing new ideas of mutual understanding, trying to understand the other. We have a long history of doing this. I remember back in 1990 when we were going through the first Intifada; the school was pro-active in bringing students, Palestinian and Israeli, together to talk about the conflict. We have received Israeli students here at

the school and we have sent our students to Israeli schools to talk to students there. And in a sense this experience was a leading experience. We have seen many different kinds of groups—intellectuals, students, university professors—forming such groups. This was very positive.

This school has always been known to be willing to be at the uppermost front of experimenting with new ideas that may not, at the very first, be very popular or accepted in the community. So it is a risk sometimes, but on the other hand, it gives hope that there are such people who are willing to endeavor.

Altogether when a family is living in the United States or the Gulf and they decide to come back to Ramallah, the first thing they think about is where are they going to send their children to school. I have seen many families who have decided to come back, and they bring their children to this school. So they are seeing this place as a place which gives hope.

Parenting is a challenge in a land that is occupied. You want to keep your children safe; you want to provide them with an education so they can succeed. Dr. Adel Yahya, is the director of PACE (Palestinian Association for Cultural Exchange) and the parent of an eighth grader at FBS. He shared the hope that keeps him in Ramallah:

"As parents you are willing to endure something [the situation] as long as my kids can go to RFS. I stayed even through the Intifada because of the school. RFS is the final resource for a significant element of society. People may have opportunities abroad but choose to stay because of RFS."

Parents choose Ramallah Friends Schools as a place to give hope, but also as a place that demands the best from their children. Students are encouraged to be free-thinkers, to gather all the facts and make their own decisions, to be open to new ideas, and to develop character based on Quaker values. Ramallah and Palestine benefit from this pool of graduates.

Joyce Ajlouny, a 1983 graduate and current RFS director, said,

> I think the Friends Schools has some credit there [in shaping Ramallah], because it has created a pool of graduates and parents who believe in such openness. When our students come here, we give them a say; we make sure their voice is heard; we train them on the importance of democracy, on the importance of equality and tolerance.

> The fact is that this is the only school in Palestine that offers a very innovative educational system. It is always renewing, always improving, stressing the importance of new methods in education and state-of-the-art type of methodology. It really stands out.

> When you see a graduate, they really have the skill set and knowledge set they need to compete with any other international students abroad. When they apply to universities in Europe or in the United States, they are at the same level, and I think that in itself is a great self-identity.

> We, living here under occupation, under bombardment, under suppression, under dispossession, you name it, all the injustices in the world are here, and

for them and our country in particular, parents live
for their kids. They save every penny so they can
make sure their kids are okay as adults.

Hope is not something that is taught, but comes from learning one's self-identity and becoming confident in one's skill levels. Hope comes from being with teachers who encourage intellectual freedom, and from a school with a long tradition of being in the forefront of academic challenges.

Holly Dhynes, FUM Field Staff from 1997-2000, says. "[RFS] is the best of Palestinian society. It offers hope for freedom and continues to be a beacon of hope."

Chapter 6
International Presence

The schools' reputation as a place of peace and tolerance in a war-torn land drew, and continues to draw, people who want to make a difference or who want to learn more about the situation as it exists in today's Middle East.

Many speakers have visited the schools and their programs have greatly impacted the students. "The way of teaching helps students to see globally," stated Reema Karam Haugen, a 1966 graduate living in Minnesota. "They [students] have a better understanding of the world. I met people from America and other cultures. We had programs and speakers from other countries, such as Helen Keller, the Russian Ballet, Duke Ellington, and other theater and drama shows. I was in the choir. There were many activities to help you grow besides studying. All of this makes you a more well-rounded person." Recently, the concerts of Israeli pianist Daniel Barenboim and the visit by Secretary of State Madeline Albright could be added to that list.

The Friends Girls School in 1889 was a boarding school that brought girls together from all over Palestine. Their teachers were from Lebanon and other staff from Ramallah. As these girls learned to live with one another, they learned that their corner of the world was very small. Customs and traditions were valuable, but one's mind could be opened to new experiences and ways of doing things. These cross-cultural experiences led the girls in the early years to learn a worldwide worldview, rather than seeing the world through provincial eyes.

Opening the school with international teachers raised the expectation that Friends Schools would always have international teachers on campus. As travel became easier, a larger international presence came through international visitors and performers.

"We have a lot of international presence on campus," stated John Hishmeh, FUM field staff from 2004-07. "International visitors come from Europe or the States all the time. We have international teachers here which other schools rarely have. That element in itself gives students a cross-cultural experience right here in their home country. And I personally value that because it fosters the idea of tolerance. It teaches tolerance in an experiential way, not a classroom way. They experience an American in class every single day so they have to learn tolerance. ... The free atmosphere and the international presence and influence are a couple of the distinguishing factors of our school that make it really special."

International Friendships

"Education of people provides hope," stated Salwa Tabri, a retired FBS music teacher. "Friends Schools are different than government schools. It opens up the world for the student, especially learning the English language and having international teachers. It opens your eyes to what is going on in the world."

Consistent international presence over the years has provided hope to students and expanded the curriculum from what other Palestinians were taught. "I made lifetime friendships," stated Reema Ali, a 1976 graduate practicing law in Falls Church, Virginia. "I learned a great deal at RFS that I would not have otherwise been exposed to if my education was restricted to the official curriculum in the West Bank, which was vetted by the Israelis and the Jordanian government at the time."

"As a Quaker growing up in Ramallah," wrote Carol Ajlouny Zaru, a 1981 graduate living in Maryland, "attending RFS shaped my identity and who I am today. The American and British teachers that taught at the Schools gave us a different perspective on education that went beyond the 'traditional' textbook methods. Due to the constant political turmoil in the region, the teachers and the students were the support systems for each other, and the bonds that were formed remain strong today. No matter where they are living today, alumni and students who even attended the Schools for a brief time are in touch and feel connected in a very powerful and beautiful bond."

Friendships are formed that may reach wider than Palestine. Before 1967, friendships reached throughout the Middle East and gave graduates the training to accept international opportunities that were available.

Lydia Simaan Dibouny/Zabaneh, a 1949 graduate, said, "RFS had a sociable influence in my life and I assume other lives because RFS joined the two sides of the River Jordan. We got to know each other more, having a lot of friends." Lydia lives in Amman, Jordan, and is retired from the Near East Council of Churches after twenty-three years as a social worker and secretary.

Another retiree is Huda Qubein Kraske, a 1960 graduate living in Washington, D.C. "I am a World Bank retiree," she wrote. "I joined the Bank in 1965 and spent many years working in Middle East and Eastern European countries. The FGS opened my eyes to the world of music, literature, philosophy, history, and the world."

More recently, relationships at the Friends Schools have been limited to other Ramallah students and teachers. They haven't been as widespread among students because of travel restrictions for Palestinians due to Israel's occupation. But the international presence of teachers and performers continues and is essential to continuing expanding students' worldwide worldview.

"International teachers are a link with the outside world," stated Allyn Dhynes, FUM field staff from 1997-2000. "[Palestinians] feel like their cause is understood by the internationals and [that] gives hope in their current situation. The most important thing is to provide person and presence in the current situation. It brings hope just by your presence. They rely on visitors and international teachers to tell the outside world of their humanity."

Every international person who visits or works at the Ramallah Friends Schools brings hope—hope that someone cares enough to come and see, hope that when they leave, they will take their message with them, and hope that, eventually, new opportunities will open for Palestinian students.

International Study

"As a graduate of FGS, I was fluent in the Arabic and English languages," wrote Wafa Rukab Atallah, a 1982 graduate living in Jacksonville, Florida. "I learned from a lot of teachers to depend on myself, love my country, be proud of being Palestinian, and to be proud that I was a graduate of FGS—even though a lot of Palestinians consider us Americanized students—but we were not."

At the Friends Boys School, high school students have opportunities to attend international conferences. For the past several years, students have gone to leadership conferences at Sidwell Friends School, Washington, D.C., and some students worked with Brooklyn Friends School (New York) on a documentary project.

The experience with the most far-ranging impact is clearly the Model United Nations conferences, which FBS students have participated since 2005. The first two years, ten students accompanied John Hishmeh, who was responsible for bringing this program to Ramallah Friends Schools. In 2007, eighteen students from RFS joined over three hundred other students for the Model United Nations program in Doha, Qatar. Each student was assigned a country and issues before the conference, and they became well read on their assignments. They engaged in dialogue and debated the most pressing international issues of the day, including the development of infrastructure in Iraq, North Korean and Iranian nuclear development, the situation in Darfur, and the freedom of the press in the Middle East.

All of these opportunities open students' minds to a worldwide worldview that is bigger than their family, community, and school. This helps to facilitate the openness to go to college away from home, a tradition that is long standing. In the early days of the Friends Boys School (1901-14), Christina Jones wrote, "a large number migrated to the United States, the first in a chain that has bound Ramallah with the United States in a remarkable way" (*Friends in Palestine*, 54).

Of the eighty-two 2006 gradates, 36.6 percent went to college in North America and 6 percent went to Europe. A total of 92 percent of the graduating class matriculated to a four-year university. John Hishmeh said, "The fact that the school has chosen to invest in preparing students for college is a great thing. And the number of scholarships for students is growing, and that makes the school unique."

In college, RFS graduates have established a record of accomplishment that speaks to the quality of their preparation. Several U.S. Quaker colleges have established Ramallah scholarships, recognizing the value added to their campuses by these students.

John spent much of his three-year term as FUM field staff working as the college counselor. He talked about this role at the school: "We are the only school in the West Bank or Gaza that has a college counselor. I am the only college counselor in this country. So what that means is that we are investing in our students' future, we are creating and facilitating opportunities for the future by managing contacts, helping them prepare, getting them college plans, and discussing all the issues. I have families from other schools who call me asking to make appointments because word spreads."

Parents in Ramallah are no different than parents elsewhere. They want only the best for their children. They try to provide better opportunities for their children than what they had. And all of this flows from the love they have for their children.

Joyce Ajlouny said:

> For parents to feel, "Wow, I am providing [my children] an excellent education and an opportunity to study abroad," it's really giving them that hope that, "I am not only providing for my kids in monetary terms, but I am also going to give them the opportunity to be something." And this is what this school does — provides hope for the families.

> Last year students went to Harvard and Stanford and MIT, and I believe it is 37 percent of our graduating students went to North America and 98 percent end up in colleges — at top universities, with full scholarships, sometimes partial, but this is the hope I think that is ingrained in Friends Schools.

> I have a lot of parents who come here. Even just two days ago someone called me and said, "I want to move my child from another school to FS. He will be in seventh grade next year. Please, please find him a place. It's very important to me. I want

him to finish the International Baccalaureate (IB) program so he can go to medical school in England. If he graduates from any other school he is not going to have that chance. His father is a doctor and so he wants to do the same."

International Impact

"I felt I gained good education from the FGS and good language skills which enabled me to be exposed to the international community," wrote Rana Bahu Toubassi, a 1988 graduate and Ramallah lawyer working with a European Union project for empowering the Palestinian Judiciary.

This fluency in both Arabic and English plays a huge role in the choices students make for further education and for life. Jacob G. Zarou, a 1980 graduate living on Long Island, New York, wrote, "One thing for sure, it made it very easy for me to live in the USA."

Since 1869, internationals have played a role in Ramallah Friends Schools and in the lives of the students they have touched. Mazen Karam, a 1971 graduate offers an example of such, "I also used to spend time with my science teacher outside of the classroom. He was from North Carolina and I used to play tennis with him. We were very close friends and also I used to work in the lab with him. That was something that other schools did not have at that time." Mazen lived in North Carolina for a time, but he and his wife Hula moved back to Ramallah so their children would have this international experience of education that they had both had.

Stephen Lassiter, a teacher at the Friends Boys School in 2007-08 from North Carolina, had his students read *The Diary of Anne Frank*. Stephen wrote,

I knew that reading the *Diary of Anne Frank* with Palestinian students would be interesting and difficult for both them and myself. While the story helps give a glimpse into the human condition and has applicable lessons no matter where it is read, the *Diary of Anne Frank* — its message, its plot and its characters — has a particular poignancy for Palestinian students. I asked my students to keep journals, not only to improve their writing skills, but also to help them process their feelings and thoughts while reading the story.

It was very difficult for many of my students to read Anne Frank — especially at the beginning of the story. They had a hard time differentiating between Jewish oppression in the 1940s and their current oppression under Israeli military occupation.

Nevertheless, many of my students empathized with Anne. They felt the expression of a shared human condition in her voice, and they came to appreciate her spirit. They admired and respected her optimism under such harsh and humiliating conditions. And many came to see Anne's radiance as an inspiration. For a people who have been displaced, oppressed and who have lived under military occupation for over 40 years, Anne represented the possibility to remain optimistic and cheerful in a seemingly hopeless situation.

Few students in the United States would be able to fathom what it is like to have an armed soldier board their bus on the way back from a class trip. Few

American students would be able to understand the feelings of having one's dignity and land taken from them. And it would be difficult for American youth to comprehend what it is like to have their movement restricted under a military occupation. But this is the reality for our students here at the Ramallah Friends Schools.

However, instead of resigning to defeatism, our students exude the same resilience as Anne. They are intelligent, vibrant and optimistic. For many of them, the *Diary of Anne Frank* was a reminder of all that they can be, an affirmation that, despite all the atrocities happening in the world, a life driven by hope, morality and determination will provide more fulfillment than one of despair and fear.

Such bold and creative education is often provided by the international teachers attracted to RFS. One should never underestimate the impact of international teachers, international performers, and international volunteers.

Joyce Ajlouny said:

I believe if you asked the students who were here in the past, who from their teachers influenced them the most, you are going to see a huge number who will say, "The international teachers influenced me the most." So this is something I am trying to achieve with the school, trying to bring them in. It is not to say that our teachers are of less quality than the internationals, but the teachers who come through FUM or who are Quakers, they come young and energetic, wanting to serve. They see injustice here and they want to do something about it and help in any way possible. They bring energy, they bring love, they bring hope, they bring creativity, they bring freshness. And this is what the community really looks for, and I believe it is them who really make the difference here. They add those extras that show the students that, "oh look, we can study this way," or "we can do a book report that way," the non-traditional ways of doing it or "we can have a summer camp to include these activities," or "we can study world religions," or "we can learn the importance of giving." It's all part of these new approaches these teachers bring, their energy, and their love. I really believe that they make a huge, huge impact here, and we need to keep them coming. This is a main issue for me. I want to keep them coming.

The American teachers who came before provided the students with a person to vent, to speak up, for someone to listen to them and be pastoral ... that was the freshness, the open-mindedness that was provided by the teachers. So many of my memories here are memories I have linked with international teachers.

Chapter 7
Compassionate Hearts

For the first time in many years, two specificly Quaker class-es were added to the ethics track in the Ramallah Friends Schools curriculum in 2007. *Quaker History* was offered to eighth graders and *Quaker Faith and Practice* to juniors.

The *Quaker History* course began with the history of FUM, focusing on Quaker schools worldwide. It was moving to witness the students learn about the conditions of students in Turkana, East Africa, who don't have desks in their classrooms. The students all wanted to adopt Turkana as a service project and raise funds for desks.

The class continued with the history of Ramallah Friends Schools and the influence of Quakers in the Middle East. Students decided to add another project — this time the Friends Play Center at the Amari refugee camp.

A field trip to the Play Center was scheduled. Students arrived at Amari to interact with the preschoolers and to hand out gifts they had purchased from their donations. At first they remained in two groups. The preschoolers sang songs and showed off their skills with the English alphabet and counted to ten in Arabic.

Blank paper and crayons were handed out and the eighth graders joined the preschoolers as they drew. Face painting ensued. There was much laughter and joy in the room. Each preschooler received a wrapped gift: coloring books for the girls and car games for the boys. They clutched their gifts to their chests and waited for permission to open them. Smiles were broad and their eyes were focused on the gift bearers.

One eighth grade boy said, "They need us to come." Several girls said, "Let's make this a yearly class project." Overall, the feeling was positive and very supportive. There is much hope for these young people with their compassionate hearts.

Example Begins Early

"One of the impacts of the Friends Schools is raising children and youth to become compassionate people," stated Joyce Ajlouny. "I talk to my students [the eighth graders taking *Quaker History*] about the importance of giving and that giving is more meaningful than receiving … You need to feel what it feels like to give. So I know they will grow up with this value."

"I enjoy fundraising for charities in the West Bank," wrote 1976 graduate Iman Odeh-Yabroudi, living in Dubai, United Arab Emirates. "We have organized an annual charity fundraiser for the past three years and look forward to our fourth event in 2008. The Palestine Youth Orchestra was the latest; it took place in Dubai, March 11, 2007, at the Dubai Community Theater. Concerts were performed to delighted audiences from all over the Emirates. We flew in thirty-five musicians from the West Bank cities of Ramallah, Bethlehem, Jerusalem, and Beit Sahour. They more than earned their stay with their talent and skill."

"What made me do that," Iman said, "is something we did in school! The collection called White Gifts. Every once in a while we were encouraged to give as little as one piaster (the Jordanian currency then) to the needy. Sharing and giving to the needy remains with me today as the White Gifts of those school days."

At Friends Girls School, Principal Diana Abdul Nour carries on the tradition begun over 100 years ago. The White Gifts program teaches compassion in the early grades. Raising money begins in the fall term with bake sales and donations from the students' pocket money. By December 2006, over $4,300 was raised, and ninty-three families in need had benefited.

"The girls school White Gift program," stated Colin South, director from 2000-04, "engaged parents as well, as they made cakes and pastries and then would sell them. The money was then used by the school for gifts for the poor and needy, especially when they went on community visits to nursing homes or orphanages."

No one seems to know the origin of the name White Gift, but the activity has left a profound impact on students in Ramallah.

"As young students, we were taken many times to perform dance or songs and help out senior citizens, blind kids, and the unfortunate," wrote Besan Al-Omary, a 2001 graduate who lives in Ramallah and works as producer/reporter for Al-Jazeera Satellite Channel. "This experience I carry with me today. At RFS they taught us compassion for the others and that is something I hope to teach my kids in the future."

Motive to Serve

One of the Quaker values taught at RFS is service, which is articulated, "To take the fullest opportunity as it arises for the use of our gifts in the service of God and the community."

In an occupied land it would be very easy to become self-centered, concerned mainly with the survival of one's self and family. "Take care of number one," may be the normal response to living in the difficult conditions of occupation, money shortages caused by the Intifada, and economic embargos (and therefore food shortages and other basic needs, etc.). Yet, through it all, Friends Schools have continued to encourage service and compassion, reaching out to the less fortunate.

Graham Leonard taught at FBS from 1950-51 and was pastor of Ramallah Friends Meeting from 1955-57. He said, "In school they are in touch with people who have no other motive than to serve." The role models students see of people from across the world, stopping their normal life and coming to serve at the Schools, leaves a lasting impression of the importance of service and compassion.

Community service teaches compassion for those less fortunate no matter what one's circumstances; there is always someone less fortunate than yourself. Focusing on others, even in the worst of times, helps build character.

"Community service always went on right through the Intifada," said Colin South. "Always there was an interest in trying to serve the community, but also to alert children to the needs and how to be responsible members of their community. This tradition, especially well established at the girls school and then at the boys school through the International Baccalaureate (IB) which requires a community service component, was that the children should be engaged with the needs of the community in one way or another."

Engagement with the Community

During the strategic planning process that was implemented when Colin South was director from 2000-04, parents, teachers, and students were interviewed and asked about the schools. The responses made it clear, according to Colin, "that parents had a concern for more engagement with the community." Several new projects resulted in the form of outreach to the community.

One was the Kaykab Gardens, which is housed at Swift House, across the street from the Friends Boys School. According to Colin,

In its vision, it was a botanical garden, but it has now become an educational garden. It was intended that this be a learning experience with a collection of Palestinian flora, which would help Palestinians with their identity as Palestinians. It would help them recognize their heritage because here are a whole host of plants that were used for medicinal purposes.

Another aspect was the organic approach—non-herbicide, non-pesticide, non-fertilized approach to growing things. A school in the United States (Moses Brown, Providence, Rhode Island) has as part of its curriculum how to farm organically. Being in touch with the land, caring for the land, supporting the land, and good stewardship of the land, is a part of Quaker witness. The whole organic idea was a reaction to the overuse of pesticides in the area, to the overuse of fertilizers in local farming in Palestine. So we were trying to educate them that they didn't need to do that.

What I see now, three years after, is a remarkable achievement. The minister of agriculture for Palestine came for a visit and was impressed.

Funded by the Heinrich Boll Foundation (Berlin, Germany), the project employs a project coordinator, educational officer, and two gardeners. People come in off the noisy, main street and eat their lunch, talk on their cell phones, or visit in small groups. Benches are available for sitting where the ever-changing flora of the garden is a welcoming change from the daily grind of life.

Last year, over 1,200 students from public, private, and United Nations Relief and Works Agency (UNRWA) schools visited the gardens for guided tours and training programs. In the 3,000 square meter facility, at least 100 different trees, shrubs, and small plants are on display, including the relatively unknown Kaykab tree.

The staff also cares for the organic garden, where seasonal fruits and vegetables are grown and sold to the community, parents, and staff.

"Kaykab Gardens also operates as an educational facility for the Friends Schools," states the RFS Web site. "Each year, science students from all grades spend time at the garden to supplement their classroom experiences. This curriculum runs parallel to their required science courses — after learning about a subject, students participate in gardening activities under the guidance of the educational coordinator and gardener. This program lasts the entire academic year and is part of a progressive curriculum."

Another project that has a profound impact on the RFS community and into the world, is the Barenboim-Said Foundation concerts which bring together musicians from Arab countries and Israel. This project has mushroomed from the first concerts held in the boys school auditorium to concerts worldwide by the East-West Divan Orchestra.

Colin South explained the beginnings: "We already had a musicians program established at Friends Schools and most of these musicians came from Germany or Austria. It began to develop an orchestra and to develop a conservatory. And that resulted while we were there in the first major concert given and most of the musicians were Friends Schools students. And Daniel Barenboim himself conducted it in 2004. The auditorium was packed. It was not just about the students, it was about the community. It was another cultural expression, another cultural element of cooperation between the school and the community."

The Mozart Festival of Israel and Palestine have played many concerts in the cities from Jerusalem and Tiberius to Ramallah. For those several hours, life seems normal and the occupation far away.

"One of the great things about the school is the number of community events that are hosted here on our campus," said John Hishmeh, FUM field staff 2004-07. "I can't think of any other school that hosts the types of community events and concerts that we do. People use our facilities here for sports and athletic events ... Events like this hosted throughout the year make this place a community center."

Service Learning Program

Students enrolled in the International Baccalaureate (IB) program must complete a certain number of community service hours in order to graduate. This part of the program reinforces the earlier learning of the students, plus moves them into the wider stream of community life. A list of projects is available for students to choose from, and they volunteer their hours helping in a variety of ways.

Students affect change in the community with their presence and help, and the community work continues to mold the lives and values of these young people.

Joyce Ajlouny said,

> Our service learning program shows them their community is not a homogenous one, it has people from all walks of life, people in need who need their support. And I always stress that giving is not always giving money, but also giving of yourself, and the importance of volunteerism.
>
> We may not influence 100 percent of our students, but if we influence a few, then we have done a good job. The impact on the character development of this community is great—we know our students are going to grow up and be the most influential people

in our community, the ones with the superb English language, the ones with the good education abroad, the ones who highlight the job market and [who] people want to employ. So it is good to know that they will be placed in these institutions and given these responsibilities with the values that have become ingrained in them. That makes us proud.

Future Rewards

A recent graduate, Amra Amra, said, "After attending Friends, I became more social and appreciative. I now am more thankful and connected with humanity. The things I used to take for granted I now cherish. I feel sorry for the millions of people who are blinded by their ignorance. This opportunity truly broadened my horizons and allowed me to be more connected to my community and heritage." Amra is majoring in finance at Birzeit University and works at the Ramallah YMCA, living out the values she learned at RFS.

Alumni stay very connected to the Friends Schools and want to continue supporting it. "We (my wife and I) believe it is important to give back to the school because we have taken so much from it," stated Issa Cook, a 1954 graduate. He now lives in Houston, Texas, after being deported following the 1967 war when he was deputy mayor of Ramallah. "We believe in giving back. Giving is something we learned there and it is very important to us." Financial support from alumni is yet another expression of the compassionate hearts fostered at RFS.

Chapter 8
Peace Builders

Farid Tabri was at the boys school almost fifty years before retiring (1919-68). He taught Arabic and was also dean. He led chapel and would read from the Bible one day and from the Koran the next. He studied Arabic in Egypt with a great Muslim religious teacher, went to college in Germany where he met his wife, and spent his life dedicated to the Friends Schools when they were boarding schools.

His daughters, Salwa and Fadwa Tabri, are also retired from the Friends Boys School. Salwa was the pianist who played accompaniment for student productions, chapel, and chorus. After teaching for a few years, she went to Germany for further musical study. She has multiple sclerosis now and is no longer able to play the piano or walk without assistance. Fadwa was the FBS librarian for twenty-five years and also taught Arabic to English-speaking students.

Salwa said, "Why don't people in America know that Christians and Muslims live together in peace? We are Christians and are surrounded by Muslims but we all live in peace and have for generations."

Salwa said, "Living under occupation is the worst." She and Fadwa then talked about how, when they lived under Jordanian rule, they all lived in peace and even carried Jordanian passports. But now, life is much harder.

During the second Intifada a shell hit the water tank on their roof top and water started pouring in on them as they were sleeping upstairs. They were able to turn the water off before too much damage was done. Another rude awakening in the middle of the night happened when the Israeli soldiers were pounding on the front door. The soldiers asked to see their identification papers and then realized they had the wrong house.

Salwa was the conductor of the Palestine chorus from Ramallah. One time they were to perform in Jerusalem, but first they all had to apply for permits. When the permits were returned, everyone had one except for Salwa, the conductor. The thinking may have been, "The chorus won't come if their conductor is denied entry." But these sisters were feisty. They used an ambulance and Salwa rode in the patient bed. They went to the checkpoint, thinking they could get her through that way. But the checkpoint was closed and after lying in the patient bed for two hours, they decided to call it quits.

They told several other stories, but what shined through was the courageous spirit of nonviolent resistance. They said, "The Israeli's want us to get on our knees and beg for mercy, but that will never happen. We will continue to carry on our daily lives and resist when we can. Our spirits will not be broken!"

The impact of the Quaker values in the Friends Schools is seen so clearly in the lives of these two Christian women. These Christians and their Muslim neighbors under occupation want to live their lives in peace.

The Quaker Way of Nonviolence

"Muslims and Christians have lived together for centuries peacefully," Joy Totah-Hilden said. Her father, Khalil Totah, was principal of the boys school for over twenty-five years, serving two different times. She continued, "RFS has a huge job as a living example to the community of another way of problem solving." She was referring to living out the peace testimony. Exploring this further, she talked about the ways that political governments try to divide people, and she concluded, "Friends, by their example and teaching, can help heal the rift."

The walls surrounding the schools carve out a safe haven, a place where students and teachers can model a peaceful way of relating to one another, a place where skills are learned and practiced.

Akel Biltaji, a 1959 graduate who is a Jordanian Senator and has been special advisor to King Abdullah II of Jordan, said,

> Friends Schools were unusual because the moment you step inside the gates, you drop the violence but maintain the cause. Friends have not at any point of time tried to convert, influence, intimidate, or infuriate any of the community.

> You know that they were the first to come out. And when you speak of Friends you are talking about American Friends. When someone asks, "What is typical of Americans in the Middle East now?" I say to them [the press], "Study the Friends."

> In the eighteenth century, the interest of the Christian communities became apparent in the Holy Lands. It was stronger in the nineteenth century when the Ottomans allowed non-Muslims to connect and associate with foreign consulates, particularly European. Americans didn't have a consulate in the Holy Land at that time so they sent missionaries and started many schools … there was a deeper motive in that; because of their presence in the Holy Land they could restore the Temple and a lot of the

Judeo-Christian influence. They were the "restorers," very much like today's Zionists.

Now to balance that we have the Mennonites and the Quakers—and they were people who were very much welcomed. They were willing to go out and give assistance, medical care, and education for Muslims and Christians alike, because they were down-to-earth humanitarians.

In Ramallah, they found that the Quaker way was a nice way of going on Sunday, keeping silent as well as singing hymns. Look at the Arab perception to the American presence now in Iraq. And look at the perception in the West Bank, because here you have a different approach to conflict because of Friends.

In the almost 140 years since Friends arrived in Ramallah, their presence has been felt. Sybil and Eli Jones planted seeds among some people and left the legacy of Hope School. The Quaker way began. Through the years and numerous occupations, the Quaker way of nonviolence remains a model, a beacon of light upon the hill.

Teaching Nonviolence

"The Quaker principles of nonviolence have been etched in my psyche and I find myself sickened by war, poverty, disease, oppression, and human rights violations. This is all due to my upbringing at Friends Girls School." These words were written by Huda Qubein Kraske, a 1960 graduate living in Washington, D.C. She studied economics at the American University in Washington, D.C., and spent her career working for the World Bank.

Siblings Michael Karam and Reema Karam Haugen both agreed on the importance of learning conflict resolution at the Friends Schools. Michael, a 1957 graduate, said, "We were taught peace and conflict resolution. Our teachers were examples." Michael is a medical doctor in Raleigh, North Carolina.

Friends Schools "teaches peace," said his sister, Reema Karam Haugen, a 1966 graduate. "Our teachers always talked about ways to resolve things peacefully." Reema is a bilingual resource teacher for K-8, and teaches workshops on bilingual education in the Dearborn, Michigan, area.

Teaching nonviolence has historically been a way that Friends have helped students and staff learn about the peace testimony. When the strategic planning process was in motion, peace was identified as a Quaker value. Quaker values were endorsed by the Board of Trustees on December 17, 2002, and peace was identified:

"To acknowledge in our lives those emotions, attitudes, and prejudices which lie at the roots of destructive conflict. To faithfully maintain our witness that war and the seeds of war are inconsistent with our understanding of the love of God. We should stand firm in this testimony even when others commit or prepare to commit acts of violence. We should acknowledge that those who do prepare for or commit acts of violence are also children of God."

Since the Quaker values were endorsed, a number of students have passed through the schools. Ayed O. Ayed is a 2005 graduate studying medicine in Amman, Jordan. During an interview in Amman, he stated, "I developed many of the beliefs and ideals I hold today during my years at RFS. I believe that we should be tolerant of other people, regardless of their beliefs and other ways in which they may differ from us. I strongly agree with peace and negotiation as tools to solve our problems rather than the use of brute force. ... Notably, my understanding of democracy, justice, creativity, and service was influenced by RFS, too."

Ayed received elements of hopeful peacebuilding through a course he took that looked at historical figures like Martin Luther King Jr., Gandhi, and other peacemakers. He vividly remembered studying Martin Luther King Jr. and the special chapel service held that related the black struggle in the United States to what was happening in Palestine. The elements that made the most impact were, "looking at nonviolent ways of fighting truth and justice and values that are important to the struggle for freedom. These experiences of others helped shape me and provided me with hope. We learned to give peace a chance, not just rush into doing something reactive."

Ayed continued, "We need reason and logic. You can't fight tanks with stones. Friends Schools helped me develop a love for my country through every Monday assembly. The moment of silence helped me to reflect on my life and my day. I can remember certain events where we talked about things—we were encouraged to talk about what was inside—what you want, what our fears are."

The chapel program and the ethics classes continue to shape the minds and hearts of the students. Quaker values become internalized during these times as students learn of the experiences of others, as well as conflict resolution skills.

Music Builds Peace
Daniel Barenboim and Edward Said

When Colin South began his time as director (2000-04), he asked himself, "How can the Ramallah Friends Schools assist the community in responding to the Intifada? How can we support the Palestinian people in this time of desperate struggle, not in terms of violent struggle, but in terms of emotional struggle and challenge?" He found the answers in artistic expression:

The idea was conceived using the Friends Schools. I looked at their Friend-in-Residence program. To expand on that idea, it seemed like a great idea, with all this stone around us, to have a sculpture using all this limestone, helping children to be creative in their response to the conflict.

There was already an active Music Conservatory in town where some of the boys and girls of the Friends Boys School had instrument tuition. Music had been taught very capably at Friends Girls School for some years. The visit of Daniel Barenboim, a Jewish Israeli and American citizen, to Friends Boys School in 2001 was, however, a turning point.

I had been thinking about an Artist-in-Residence program so that an artist could work with the children of our schools to help them express their feelings creatively in these very difficult circumstances. In discussion with Daniel, he decided to see what he could do. Out of this grew an amazing program of professional musicians from Germany and Austria who were based at the Friends Boys School. They encouraged first our children, then, in association with the Conservatory, students in other schools, to play music rather than pass music examinations. They wanted to encourage children to have a passion for music rather than only be technically proficient. The upshot of this program, supported by the Barrenboim-Said foundation, was the establishment of the first Youth Orchestra in Ramallah, the first concert of which was conducted in the FBS

Khalil Totah Hall by Daniel Barenboim himself in
2004. The auditorium was packed.

Sam Bahour reported on the event in *Live from Palestine*, on
May 7, 2004. Sam is a Palestinian American businessman living
in El-Bireh. He wrote:

> Mr. Barenboim, this absolutely incredible musi-
> cian—a legend in his own right—took to the stage
> tonight at the Friends Boys School in front of a
> standing room only audience and proceeded to per-
> form an extraordinary piano recital. ...
>
> ... As if a piano recital was not enough, Mr. Baren-
> boim proceeded to proudly announce that an ini-
> tiative that he and the late Dr. [Edward] Said
> started during their last trip in August of last year,
> the desire to create a Palestinian Orchestra within
> five years, had already begun to bud. He spoke as
> two dozen Palestinian youth music students from
> the National Conservatory of Music Student Or-
> chestra—or more accurately called tonight by Mr.
> Barenboim, the Palestine Youth Orchestra—sur-
> rounded him on stage, each armed with a weapon
> of mass pleasure, violins, flutes, cellos, and drums.
> This beginning Palestinian orchestra performed for
> the first time tonight under the directive of con-
> ductor Daniel Barenboim. They were received by
> multiple standing ovations and by Mr. Barenboim's
> beaming pride and joy.

The Palestine Youth Orchestra has become the East-West
Divan Orchestra which incorporates Arab and Israeli students

into the program. Rehearsals are in Spain and the orchestra travels on Spanish passports as they play concerts throughout the Arab and Israeli world.

This initiative began at the Ramallah Friends Schools, and an excellent music program continues for the students. In April 2007, the Palestine Mozart Festival had three performances at Friends Schools. The Festival was held in different locations and some performances were also in Jerusalem. One night was choral and chamber classics night with world renowned musicians, the London (England) Choir, and the Jerusalem (Ramallah) Chorus, plus an orchestra that included some Friends Schools students.

These musical concerts were "not just about the students," concluded Colin. "It was about the community. It was another cultural expression, another cultural element of cooperation between the school and the community. It was about cooperation and community and Daniel Barenboim and Edward Said's vision of reconciliation and understanding through music. The fruits of this work can be found in the refugee camps around Ramallah, in many of the schools of the West Bank and in Israel itself."

Peace Builders

There have certainly been many opportunities for people to build peace. Going back to the 1967 war, a number of people described what it was like during that time, and how the Quaker way of peacemaking impacted what happened to them.

Samia Ajlouny, a 1969 graduate living in California, said,

> Our life was involved with politics as kids. We thought that there was going to be something—a war, because there was an atmosphere of war.

We had an Arabic teacher, Ms. Fares. She was one of the best teachers because she did not just come to class, teach, and go. She would give us ten minutes of her class for an open discussion, where if you had any questions and if she was able to answer it, she would. She respected ... Nasser, the President of Egypt, during the 1967 war, and to all of us he was the idol of the Arab [nation]. He was a strong leader.

So we asked, "Ms. Fares, we are afraid. We heard there is going to be a war." As I remember this, the hair on my arms is just standing up. She looked at us and she said, "Afraid of what? To die? That's fine. If you die with the people, with everyone, it is a blessing from God that you do not die by yourself." There is a word in Arabic, death with people, with a group, is a blessing. "So why are you afraid? Don't be afraid, be strong, and we will have our culture back someday."

Ramallah before the war was nicer—it was like a heaven. It was beautiful, it was a summer resort; you could walk peacefully even after dark until nine o'clock at night. You could hear music everywhere.

Then after the war, all that was just gone. No more Emirates for the summer, everything stopped. There was a fear not to go out at night. Just go to school, come home, and absolutely no going out at night. Our social life stopped. I was sixteen years old. There was no electricity after the war, so we used

gasoline lanterns and candles to study by. Parents
would say, "Don't complain. You can still study."
And sometimes we would have to cover the window, especially during the war and right after. They
[soldiers] used to walk around—and we could hear
their footsteps—to see if we were inside the house.
My sister sent my mother a big Mother's Day card
from the United States and we used it to cover the
candle so it would not give any direct light to the
window.

As a Palestinian, and growing up here during the
war, I was always afraid. When I moved to the
U.S., I would say I was from the southern states
and that is why I have an accent. But after awhile I
said to myself, "I have to stand for what I am." Here
I am—a peaceful person, a Palestinian. I don't carry a gun; we are peaceful and we always believe in
solving problems peacefully, whether it is politically
in our country or even at work when I have clashes
with co-workers. You always solve the problem
peacefully.

The impact of the school is seen in my work. At
my review, my boss said, "Since you came here, everything is calm, and there is more teamwork. You
have helped people to forget their differences and
work together." And I said to them, "Remember I
spent fourteen years with the Quakers."

Dr. George Atalla Assousa, a 1953 graduate, lives in London,
England. He wrote about the influence of the Schools in making his professional decisions: "I was introduced to Quakers in

Ramallah, and attending Friends Boys School was critical to the direction my life took, both professionally and in personal, social commitments. For over thirteen years (1973-86), I devoted significant amounts of my time to several initiatives which I either started or co-started, such as FAIR (Foundation for Arab Israeli Reconciliation), SIAS (Salzburg International Affairs Seminar), TIDE (Trust for International Development and Education), and COPSED (Council for Palestinian Social and Economic Development) in the U.S. and Europe. In following years, I was less actively contributing in other ways, such as the Qattan Foundation. These efforts and initiatives have been in support of the Palestinian social, economic, and educational development in the West Bank, and to approaches to conflict resolution."

Another graduate who also works to change the perceptions others have of Palestinians, is Mona Hasan, a 1998 graduate now living in Durham, North Carolina. She wrote, "Today I am in advertising in hopes of using my skills and industry connections to raise awareness for the Palestinian situation. Every now and then I begin telling people about where I come from and how I grew up, and I completely change their perception of the Palestinian people. And I hope down the road, I could work to do more."

The number of Palestinians living outside Palestine who are working for nonviolent change is enormous. But there are also many alumni who remain in the Palestinian community and live lives of nonviolent resistance and change.

"Maybe someone should make a study about this," Mahmoud Amra, the head of FBS and a 1979 graduate stated, "the idea of having people who are politically or socially promoting the idea of nonviolent struggle against the occupation. Many of those people are graduates of the school. And this would mean to me that the principles of Quakerism have begun to be accepted by different organizations who have adopted such ideas, that there are other ways to struggle and to solve conflict without using violence. And if we look closer to these organizations, we could see people who have been students at Friends Schools or associated with the school in one way or the other. I believe this has had a great impact. So now if you tried to make a survey of students in the school, I believe you would find the majority of students who believed in this particular principle of nonviolence."

The Schools make another contribution to international peacemaking through hosting international workcamps. For many years, FUM has sponsored a summer work/study experience in Ramallah hosted by the Friends Schools and coordinated by boys school math teacher, Mohammad Saleem. During these work experiences, participants volunteer at the Schools in a variety of tasks and meet with local political, religious, peace, and social figures; enjoy the hospitality of Palestinian families; worship with the Friends community; learn about the activities of the Friends International Center in Ramallah (housed at the recently renovated meetinghouse); visit the Friends Play Center in the Amari refugee camp; and similarly visit in Israel and support the work of peace groups.

Chapter 9
Enduring Hope

Hope is foundational for the continuing presence of the Ramallah Friends Schools as evidenced in the family tradition to attend Friends Schools and the enduring friendships that are maintained through life.

Family Tradition

Many families have a tradition of attending Ramallah Friends Schools. There are the longstanding Quaker families like the Ajlounys and the Zarus. There are Christian families in the community like the Karams and the Khalafs. There are Muslim families like the Armas and Hamoudys.

"I am very proud to have graduated from Friends," wrote Maria Lisa Araj Mufareh, a 1997 graduate living in Baltimore, Maryland. "My great-uncle, Dr. Khalil Totah, was the principal of Friends. My father attended Friends as well, and it has a longstanding history in my family. Because I grew up in the States and moved to Ramallah when I was fourteen, and with the education I received at Friends, I believe it helped me get into one of the best universities in the States. I am a strong and independent individual today, and I believe Friends had a lot to do with it."

Maria continued, "And the bonds of friendships I made were and are memorable. I keep in touch with many classmates as they tell me who they got married to, where they live, and how many children they have! … It's so great to know that those friends shared the same experiences I did, and we always have those memories to fall back on. They are lifelong friends."

Other students recalled the importance of family tradition. Huda Qubein Kraske, a 1960 graduate living in Washington, D.C., wrote, "My life would not have been the same had I not attended the Friends Girls School for eight years (1952-60). My mother, sister, and several of my uncles and cousins had earlier attended the Friends Schools."

"As the son of an RFS student, Qustandi Karam, the brother of six RFS graduates, and husband of RFS graduate, Hula, there is no limit to the stories I can tell," stated Mazen Karam, a 1971 graduate living in Ramallah. "The special relation between the school and its former students helped me stay close to the school and made me and my wife move back to Ramallah so that our children could attend the same school that we and my father attended. I am proud to have one graduate in 2003 and two more to graduate in 2008 and 2009. I can feel that, while many things have changed at the school, the education my children are getting is similar to what I got." Mazen's five brothers and one sister all live and work in the United States.

"As a Quaker growing up in Ramallah," wrote Carol Ajlouny Zaru, a 1981 graduate living in Maryland, "attending RFS shaped my identity and who I am today … No matter where they are living today, alumni and students who even attended the school for a brief time are in touch and feel connected in a very powerful and beautiful bond."

Most students come from the Ramallah area, but some, like Ghada Dahir, move from the United States and enter school at Friends because of family tradition. She wrote, "I left the USA when I was seven years old. My parents took all four of us, my two sisters and brother, to what they called our 'home.' Upon arriving in Palestine, all sorts of crazy things went through my mind, like what in the world are we doing here! It was only after we were enrolled in the Friends Schools, did everything seem to be better than alright."

Ghada continued, "I was there from 1979-89, just one year short of graduating. Unfortunately, the political situation there was uneasy, so I was forced to leave by my parents to come back to the U.S. where my brother and sister were now attending college. Leaving Palestine was hard enough, but leaving FGS was simply unbearable. It was there that I made true friends. ... All my close friends today are ones I met during my ten year time at FGS. My best friend today is from FGS as well, and we see each other whenever we can."

Another student to move to Ramallah and attend Friends Schools was Amra Amra, a 2003 graduate, now living in El-Bireh while attending Birzeit University.

Amra wrote,

> The Friends Schools was a major impact in my life. I moved to Palestine my junior year of high school, after living my whole life in the U.S. I truly despised the thought of moving to a new country, making new friends, learning a new language, and going to a new high school. That was every sixteen-year-old's worst nightmare."

> My first months at the Friends was truly different and a new experience. As the days passed, I would try and comprehend and grasp the fact that this was my new home and school. I had to get used to it. Even though I felt like an outsider at first, I eventually grew to love my school and my classmates. I learned that the bonds created would never break. Even though we may have all gone our separate

ways, we still keep in touch and ask about one another, something that is quite uncommon in other places. I am thankful that I was given the opportunity to attend such a school that would impact me in a way I truly never imagined.

Pride becomes part of the family tradition to attend RFS. Ramzi A. Nuri, a 1977 graduate, wrote, "To make a long story short, I'll start addressing the issue of pride." Ramzi lives in Dubai, United Arab Emirates, and is a business development manager for a food manufacturer. He continued:

"We, as the Nuri family, i.e., father, brother, and I, are/were proud to be a member of the alumni of RFS. I consider Friends Schools to be the best school in Palestine. The culture, the heritage, the history that Friends Schools hold is unmatched by any other educational institution in Palestine. The building at FBS tells 1,001 words. It is more than a painting in our minds. In reality, it holds a true history of happiness, suffering, frustration, pride, achievement, and, of course, a high standard of education. Had I been living in Ramallah now, I can assure you my children would be attending Friends Schools ... certainly times have changed, new generations have been introduced, but the school remains as large as a portrait in our minds."

Enduring Friendships

Hand in hand with the family tradition of attending Friends Schools is the enduring friendships alumni make that are forged in school relationships. Some were boarding students before the 1967 war; others endured the hardships of occupation following. But when alumni meet, the bond of friendship through their Friends Schools experiences trumps all else.

"The Ramallah Friends Schools create an everlasting bond," wrote Saleem F. Zaru, a 1977 graduate living in Mt. Airy, Maryland, "not only between friends, classmates, and teachers. This magical bond goes far beyond that. It is not uncommon to see people that have attended RFS fifty years apart meet for the first time and start talking about the 'good old days at RFS', as if they were best friends all along. It is a tradition, a piece of history almost inseparable from the history of Ramallah and Palestine."

Other alumni stated the same experiences. "All the friendships I maintain were started in RFS," stated Akel Biltaji, a 1959 graduate living in Amman, Jordan. "The other day I was in Chicago and I met an alumnus from 1962. After five minutes we were repeating the same jokes and antidotes as if we had never been parted."

Ahmed Kasem Abu Kafieh, a 1952 graduate, lives north of Ramallah and is a retired chemical engineer. He wrote, "I still maintain contact with some of my friends in the U.S. and when we talk or occasionally get together we do nothing but reminisce about FBS days and adventures."

A more recent graduate is Besan Al-Omary, from 2001. He lives in Ramallah and is a producer/reporter for Al-Jazeera Satellite Channel. He wrote, "As for friendship, most of my classmates from RFS will be attending my wedding this summer (2007). We have been divided around the world, but we reunite whenever possible. This friendship is everlasting. Most of them I have known since kindergarten, and no matter how hard I look for new friends, these are the ones who always win out. The friendships we made at RFS are so valuable; our class was always filled with laughter and comedy."

Reunions play a part in keeping connections strong and in renewing friendships. Anwar Hasan Yabroudi who attended Friends Schools from 1959-67, had to leave at the beginning of the 1967 war. He lives in Dubai, United Arab Emirates, and wrote, "Regardless of our backgrounds, and even though some of us did not graduate from Friends, there is a unique sense of brotherhood and sisterhood for all Friends students. Moreover, just mentioning attending Friends gives one a feeling of prestige. Being married to a Friends graduate certainly helped. The last Friends reunion in Dubai was the best event I ever attended; it made attendees realize we belong to something."

Another Dubai graduate (1976) is Iman Odeh-Yabroudi, who wrote, "The extension of my friendship from my school days remains a big part of my social life even today. The instant connection I make with any of my classmates after years of separation is very touching."

Joyce Ajlouny, when asked about this special kind of relationship, responded:

> I hear that time and time again. That when graduates get together, they automatically click. And I can't explain it well. There is something there that bonds them, that makes them friends immediately. And when I was in Florida last year for the Ramallah convention, we had several Friends graduates there, and in the hotel lobby I could see them caucusing around each other. None of them were my classmates—some younger, some older—but we were best buddies.
>
> When I went to Dubai for the alumni fundraising, I saw these businessmen who were our graduates, who were very well established leaders, and when I talked with them, we were friends because they shared something with me, being a Friends graduate. So there is that "click," and I think this is what made the Dubai event such a big hit, that people felt, especially those in the diaspora [dispersed people], they felt something brought them together, being a Friends alumni connected them together. They felt

they belonged somewhere—other than being Palestinian—but the Friends Schools brought them together and they started reminiscing. You could really see that bond very strongly. ...

... There is a love for the school; they really love their school. They are so grateful for it, and you can see that when one of our graduates of thirty years ago stops in to visit with little kids with them. "Hi, I brought the kids to see my school." I get this all the time, especially in the summer when people come here to visit family and then bring their kids to show them their school. Their school is like their second home.

Best School in Palestine

"RFS is tops, educationally, in Palestine," stated Retha Mc-Cutchen, director from 1995-97. "Students need this education for hope outside of this community. Many students go to universities all over the world. It seems hopeless here; in the place they go to university, there is hope for something else to do."

Dr. Adel Yahya is the director of PACE (Palestinian Association for Cultural Exchange). He is also the parent of an eighth grader at FBS and another who will soon be old enough to go to Friends Schools. He said,

In an active sense, for good or bad, Friends Schools is the best school in the country. It is regrettable that the educational systems are collapsing and decaying. Over the past seven years, the level of education in the government schools has decayed. They have been closed for two-thirds of this past year, because of strikes, lack of funding, and salary disputes. But RFS have kept the level of education stable. They have remained open and continue to offer a high level of education.

The parents of students at RFS are happy that their child is going to that particular school. It is regrettable that not all people can afford to send their children to private schools. But if you care about your children, you care about their education and ensure that they get a good education. This would not be possible without the Quakers.

As parents, you are willing to endure something [the situation] as long as my kids can go to RFS. Even through the Intifada I stayed because of the school. RFS is the final resource for a significant element of society. People may have opportunities abroad, but choose to stay because of RFS.

Allyn Dhynes, FUM field staff and teacher from 1997-2000, stated, "Friends Schools is in a community caught between occupation, which makes education more difficult. The school offers hope amid the occupation and is known as the best."

"Parents see education as a way to provide their child with a better future in Palestine. Parents rely on the institution and it is an institution in the community in the classical sense for good. It has raised up many leaders in Palestinian society."

One of those leaders is Akel Biltaji, a 1959 graduate living in Amman, Jordan. He has had a varied career as a teacher and airline executive before entering Jordanian government service. As minister of tourism and antiquities, he was instrumental in uncovering the site used by John the Baptist to baptize Jesus.

He was the founding chief commissioner of the Aquaba Special Economic Zone. He served as special advisor to King Abdullah II and now is a member of the Jordanian Senate.

Akel stated, "Ramallah Friends Schools is more than a school; it is a way of life. I was taught critical thinking, open-mindedness, accepting others, and community work. It was because of these values that I am who I am today. They allowed us to look for mentors who taught us leadership, communication, tolerance, sports, and academic skills. It was more than a school; it was a second home."

But another aspect of the quality education is what some people see as a leadership drain in the country. "I don't know a Friends School graduate who is workless or who doesn't have opportunities," stated Mahmoud Arma, a 1979 graduate and head of Friends Boys School. "In fact, some people see that as a negative, because students have opportunities outside Palestine in other countries, and they see that as losing leaders."

"I don't think that this is something negative. I believe that they can act as an ambassador for their country and their people. I would like them to come back here, but people have different circumstances and Palestinians are all over the world."

And not only are Palestinians all over the world, but also people who have served at the Friends Schools. "The greatest impact in the world," stated Joy Totah-Hilden, "is the number of people who have served here and gone back home to speak about Ramallah Friends Schools."

Enduring Hope

Ziad Khalaf, a 1974 graduate, ticks off on his fingers the five pillars that have maintained him in the harsh environment of Ramallah since 1967. They are: love of country, his immediate family of Joyce Ajlouny and their three children, his extended family, his work at the A.M. Qattan Foundation, and the Ramallah Friends Schools. Over thirty-five members of his extended family are Friends Schools graduates. He said, "Can you imagine Ramallah without the Friends Schools? It is the most important institution in town. Everywhere you find Friends Schools graduates working hard for change. It is definitely a place of hope, where the future is being molded; there is space for expression and to respect differences."

"The stepping stones that the Friends Schools laid, you can see in Ramallah. Other schools academically follow the lead of Friends School. The school liberated the town on a social level because of the importance given to females in a patriarchical society. Other teacher training schools began to spring up. Within one hundred years, Ramallah became the educational hub of Palestine."

Graham Leonard was a teacher at FBS for one year in 1950-51 and served as pastor of Ramallah Friends Meeting from 1955-57. "Ramallah is the capital of Palestine," he said, "and the cultural center because of the presence of Friends Schools." He then emphatically asked, "Can you imagine what Ramallah would be like without the Friends Schools?"

"It is a great place," stated John Hishmeh, FUM field staff from 2004-07. "Being here for three years has been amazing. It's an amazing place and lots of good things are happening on hundreds of different levels. And at the same time, it is a hard place, it is very difficult. We have lots of problems. But in the end the good things here outweigh the bad things. And that is what we want. At least we are moving in the right direction."

"Loving our students," said Diana Abdul Nour, principal of Friends Girls School, "is the most important thing we do. Children cannot learn if they don't feel loved. There is no end to our loving a student, but at the same time, there is discipline."

Loving children is a key to the success of the Friends Schools. Parents also try to provide a normal environment for their children in their homes. They laugh with them, play with them, and love them, even though they are worried and hear gunfire at night. Dr. Adel Yahya, director of PACE, explained how this has become so normal for Palestinian families:

> It is because the parents are living for the child, not for themselves. If you were living for yourself, life would not be worth living, as an individual. But when you have an obligation to someone else, that is what keeps me going.
>
> When I wake up, I do not think about my work, the papers I am writing, the projects I am doing. When I wake up in the morning, I think about my obligation to my children, to my little son, to my daughter whom I need to take to school. My life revolves around my family. I would stop trying and have no incentive without my children.
>
> It is the family network that protects us and gives us hope—the close circle of parents, children, and friends. When people come to visit in the summer, it raises our spirits because you feel a sense of normality again.
>
> Our quality of life is not worth living. We don't know when it will end. If there is a light at the end of the tunnel, it gives you hope. But we see no light at the end of the tunnel as for seven years the world has turned its back on us. We are losing hope that this will not be permanent nor end somehow.

The light at the end of the tunnel was an expression Samia Ajlouny, a 1969 graduate living in California, also used. She said,

"My spirit, which I learned from the school, was that there is always a light at the end of the tunnel and I always use that. For a while I was very, very sick, and what helped me through was, I would always say, 'I'll be okay. This is just temporary.' Now if the pressure is too much, it is just temporary. We'll look back and say, 'It was nothing to worry about.' I endure life now for a better future. This is something I learned growing up at Friends Schools."

Hope has endured through fourteen decades of constant change, shaping the teaching staff, undergirding the Quaker values, and spreading into the community. Ramallah Friends Schools are a beacon of hope, an educational oasis in a thirsty land, a root sunk deep into the bedrock of the land.

Ayed O. Ayed, a 2005 graduate, said,

Hope is alive. And we are enduring as much as we can.

I have a love for the land, the olive trees, the mountains, my house and family, my traditions. This sense of belonging gives you something to live for. The landscape of the soul is binding.

I truly believe that peace and nonviolence are the only way of solving problems, and is the only way that brings hope. It is my true conviction, but I must play my part by putting things into action. You can't just talk; you must do your part.

When you go to Jerusalem you can notice the harmony of all faiths. We must learn to live as one country, or as two countries side-by-side. There are elements in both sides who are trying to stop this from happening. But I ask, "Give peace a chance. See how peace can work."

Appendix A
Quaker Values Endorsed by Board of Trustees

STATEMENT OF SCHOOL VALUES
AND THEIR IMPLICATIONS

TRUTH:

To be honest and truthful in all that we say and do. This challenge ranges over the management of our financial affairs, our tax obligations to government, our dealing with the law in our community and in all the words that we use in writing or in speech in our communication with others. We should not allow the strength of our convictions to betray us into making statements that are not true or are unfair.

SIMPLICITY:

To live simply is not to buy what we do not need or cannot afford. This challenge is based on the principle of leading a life free of ostentation and unnecessary luxury. This relates to proper .stewardship of the world's resources, conserving those resources, valuing them and using them when required and only out of necessity. This embodies a concern for the effects of our personal and collective behavior on the global economy and on our environment.

PEACE:
To acknowledge in our lives those emotions, attitudes and prejudices which lie at the roots of destructive conflict. To faithfully maintain our witness that war and the seeds of war are inconsistent with our understanding of the love of God. We should stand firm in this testimony even when others commit or prepare to commit acts of violence. We should acknowledge that those who do prepare for or commit acts of violence are also children of God.

EQUALITY:
To behave towards others as we would expect others to behave towards us. This principle has within it no discrimination between gender, race, economic class or social position. There should be no special treatment afforded to any person that would not be afforded to another unless there are open and transparent reasons for so doing. We stand by the testimony of marriage as a union between one man and one woman each equal before God.

TOLERANCE:
To respect the diversity among us in our lives and relationships. We should refrain from making judgments about the life journeys of others. This implies that all individuals should be accorded freedom of belief and expression in political, social and religious matters. We should expect individuals to speak their mind even if we find that uncomfortable. We will need to examine ideas that we disagree with or find difficult or challenging, and express our own point of view openly and honestly. We should not be afraid of disagreement and should not let any disagreement cause us to behave badly towards another, but accept it as an example of our diversity. We should trust that God is Love and Truth and his work in us over time will find agreement among us.

SERVICE:
To take the fullest opportunity as it arises for the use of our gifts in the service of God and the community. We should use this injunction wisely. It is not required of us that we should be constantly busy. It may be wise to cease our service activity or to change the direction of our service completely. We should be guided by God's will for us and attend to what Love requires of us.

CREATIVITY:
To live our lives in such a way that we are open to inspiration and new ideas which challenge the way we think and act. We should explore God's world, acknowledging that our journeys in it could always go further than the boundaries that we set ourselves. There is inspiration to be found all around us, in the natural world, in the sciences and the arts, in our work and in our friendships, in our sorrows as well as our joys. We should be open to new ideas from whatever sources they may come but we should also approach all new ideas with discernment seeking to enrich and understand our lives together in all that we do. Listen to the promptings of love and truth in our hearts.

DISCIPLINE:
To be disciplined and respectful in our behavior towards others and in the exercise of our responsibility towards our family and community. To employ the disciplines of reasoned argument and logical process to problem solving, recognizing that reason and logic are important tools in understanding our universe. To know when to exercise sensitivity, creativity and lateral thinking in relation to others and the world around us. To respect our bodies, knowing that we are God's creation.

JUSTICE:

To so order our lives that we expect a just and compassionate community in the life of the Schools. We seek to banish fear and to encourage a sense of security. We seek to promote a sense of belonging and group responsibility, particularly when disruptive behavior in the classroom, corridors or playground occurs or when behavior that damages good relationships between people needs correction. We also wish, as a community, to welcome behavior that supports and encourages growth towards the ideals of the Schools.

Endorsed by the Board of Trustees
December 17, 2002

Research Methodology

The following is the questionnaire that was e-mailed to all alumni and staff on the Ramallah Friends Schools e-mail list.

Questionnaire for *Enduring Hope:*
The Impact of the Ramallah Friends Schools
By Patricia Edwards-Konic

Name_____

E-mail address_____

Telephone number_____

When did you attend RFS?

Did you graduate?   What year?

What did you do right after graduation?

Where are you living today?

What are you doing today?

Please share any stories about your experience with RFS and its impact on your life and influence in the community you live in, such as the influence of a specific teacher, an incident that made an impact on you, the bonds of friendship over time, etc.

In what other ways has RFS influenced your life and community?

Instead of writing your story, would you be willing to be interviewed for this book project?

Twenty-nine questionnaires were returned. Thirty interviews were conducted plus many casual conversations. All information was read, sorted by categories, and placed within chapters. Not all information collected was used.

Appendix C
Statistics for Graduating Seniors, 2004-2006

These statistics were compiled by John Hishmeh, FUM field staff.

Class of 2004 — 53 graduates

86.8 % attended 4-year universities (46 students)
7.5 % attended 2-year universities (4 students)
3.8% did not matriculate to a university (2 students)
1.9% unreported (1 student)
      23 students to Birzeit (43.4%)
      3 students to Europe (5.7%)
      13 students to Middle East (24.5%)
      11 students to U.S. (20.8%)
      2 students did not matriculate (3.7%)
      1 unreported (1.9%)

Class of 2005 — 66 graduates

83.3% attended 4-year universities (55 students)
9.1% attended 2-year universities (6 students)
6.1% did not matriculate to a university (4 students)
1.5% unreported (1 student)
      27 students to Birzeit (40.9%)
      1 student to Canada (1.5%)
      4 students to Europe (6.1%)

13 students to Middle East (19.7%)
16 students to U.S. (24.2%)
4 students did not matriculate (6.1%)
1 student unreported (1.5%)

Class of 2006 — 82 graduates

91.5% attended 4-year universities (75 students)
3.65% attended 2-year universities (3 students)
1.2% did not matriculate to a university (1 student)
3.65 % unreported (3 students)
    28 students to Birzeit (34.1%)
    5 students to Europe (6.1%)
    15 students to Middle East (18.3%)
    30 students to U.S. (36.6%)
    1 student did not matriculate (1.2%)
    3 students unreported (3.7%)

Colleges where FBS graduates matriculated from 2004-06

Ahlia College of Jordan (3)
Akron University, Ohio
American University-Jenin (4)
American University of Beirut (4)
American University in Cairo (7)
American University of Sharjah, UAE
Academy of Art, Egypt
Birzeit University (77)
Boston University, Massachusetts
Bryn Mawr College, Pennsylvania
Butler University, Indiana
Cardiff University, United Kingdom
Case Western Reserve University, Ohio
Centre College, Kentucky
Chrisfield University, California

City University, London
College of San Mateo, California
Concordia University, Canada
Diablo Valley College, California
Earlham College, Indiana (5)
East Carolina University, North Carolina
Elon University, North Carolina
Florida State University
Guilford College, North Carolina (6)
Harvard University, Massachusetts
Hebrew University, Jerusalem
Indiana University
Jordan University (4)
Kingston University, London
Lebanese American University, Beirut
Lee University, Tennessee
Manchester Community College, New Hampshire
Massachusetts College of Pharmacy
Massachusetts Institute of Technology (2)
McGill University, Canada
Moraine Valley Community College, Chicago
New York Institute of Technology, Amman, Jordan (3)
North Carolina State University
Occidental College, California
Ohio State University (3)
Orange County Community College, California
Purdue University, Indiana
San Francisco State University, California
San Francisco Technology College, California
School of Arts, London
School of Science and Technology, Jordan (5)
Simmons College, Massachusetts (2)
Skyline College, California (2)
Stanford University, California
State University of New York
Swansea University, Wales
University of Abu Deis

University of Akron, Ohio
University of Bern, Switzerland
University at Buffalo, New York
University of Illinois, Champaign
University of Iowa (2)
University of Jordan (2)
University of Music, Germany
University of Nottingham, United Kingdom
University of Oregon, Oregon
University of Ottawa, Canada
University of Tampa, Florida
University of Texas, Austin
University of Toronto, Canada
University of Vienna, Austria
University of Wisconsin, Wisconsin
Utrecht University, Netherlands
Vienna College, Uganda
Weill Cornell Medical College, Doha, Qatar

Patricia Edwards-Konic, Author

As Friend in Residence for the spring 2007 term, Patricia Edwards-Konic conducted interviews and researched the impact of the Ramallah Friends Schools. This book is the result of those interviews and research.

As a recorded Friends minister, Patricia has pastored in Rocky Mountain, Wilmington, Iowa, and Indiana Yearly Meetings, traveled in ministry in several countries, and worked as editor of *Quaker Life* magazine for seven years and as editor of Friends United Press for two years. She currently lives in Colorado near her family.

Max Carter, Contributing Editor

Max L. Carter is the director of Friends Center and campus ministry coordinator at Guilford College in Greensboro, North Carolina, and a recorded Friends minister in North Carolina Yearly Meeting (Friends United Meeting). A product of a Quaker farming community in Indiana, his alternative service as a conscientious objector during the Vietnam War took him to teach at the Friends Boys School in Ramallah shortly after Israel's occupation of the West Bank in 1967. Following his two-year stay, he completed a degree in campus ministry at Earlham School of Religion (Richmond, Indiana), served on staff at Earlham College (Richmond, Indiana), and completed a Ph.D. at Temple University (Philadelphia, Pennsylvania) in American religious history while teaching in two of Philadelphia's Quaker secondary schools.

With his wife, Jane, he leads annual work/study trips for Friends United Meeting to Israel and Palestine to volunteer at the Ramallah Friends Schools and support the work of Israeli and Palestinian peace communities. They have three children, Maia (also a two-year veteran teacher of the Ramallah Friends Schools), Lissa, and Seth.

Printed in the United States
136433LV00002B/2/P